KID CONFIDENT

#4

How to
NAVIGATE
Middle School

KID CONFIDENT #4

How to NAVIGATE Middle School

by Anna Pozzatti, PhD, & Bonnie Massimino, MEd
illustrated by DeAndra Hodge

Magination Press · Washington, DC · American Psychological Association

To all middle schoolers, past, present, and future—*AP and BSM*

To Anna, Rebekah, and Lincoln, my best friends since middle school. Thank you for making me who I am today—*DH*

Books for Kids From the American Psychological Association

Magination Press is a registered trademark of the American Psychological Association. Order books at maginationpress.org or call 1-800-374-2721.

Series editor: Bonnie Zucker, PsyD
Book design by Rachel Ross
Printed by Lake Book Manufacturing, Inc., Melrose Park, IL

Library of Congress Cataloging-in-Publication Data
Names: Pozzatti, Anna, author. | Massimino, Bonnie, author. | Hodge, DeAndra, illustrator.
Title: How to navigate middle school / by Anna Pozzatti, & Bonnie Massimino; illustrations by DeAndra Hodge.
Description: Washington, DC: Magination Press; American Psychological Association, 2023. | Series: Kid confident book; 4 | Includes bibliographical references. | Summary: "How to handle the increasing academic demands of middle school, organizational skills and time management, how to be self-determined, have grit, and a sense of agency"—Provided by publisher.
Identifiers: LCCN 2022032939 (print) | LCCN 2022032940 (ebook) | ISBN 9781433838224 (hardback) | ISBN 9781433838231 (ebook)
Subjects: LCSH: Study skills—Juvenile literature. | Time management—Juvenile literature. | Academic achievement—Juvenile literature. | Middle school students—Juvenile literature. | BISAC: JUVENILE NONFICTION / Social Topics / Emotions & Feelings | JUVENILE NONFICTION / Health & Daily Living / General
Classification: LCC LB1049 .P69 2023 (print) | LCC LB1049 (ebook) | DDC 371.30281—dc23/eng/20220810
LC record available at https://lccn.loc.gov/2022032939
LC ebook record available at https://lccn.loc.gov/2022032940

Manufactured in the United States of America

10 9 8 7 6 5 4 3 2 1

CONTENTS

DEAR READER
(DON'T SKIP THIS!)

*Y*ou might be at the beginning of your middle school journey, or already be in middle school. Either way, you probably have some questions about what to expect and how to navigate the new demands. We don't know each other (yet), but if you are holding this book in your hands right now, we already know something about you—you are ready to be more independent and take control of your middle school experience.

Take a minute to think about your middle school concerns, hopes, and wishes.

- What are you looking forward to in middle school this year?

- What are some new activities you might want to try this school year?

- When faced with challenges, do you feel like you can grow and improve from them, or do you find yourself getting stuck?

- Do you sometimes feel stressed or pressured and have a hard time handling it?

- Do you already have good studying habits and know how to be organized?

- Do you have worries about having many teachers or more work than before?

- If you are just starting middle school, are you concerned about finding your way around the school building and switching classes?

Although this book is about middle school, it's not just about academics. We'll also focus on bigger picture topics like the best ways to think and act as you navigate the exciting journey of middle school. We'll talk about a whole bunch of interesting and useful stuff, like **MINDSET, GRIT, POSITIVE THINKING, LEARNING STYLES, MANAGING STRESS AND PRESSURE**, and more! Our biggest goal for you is that you will learn some things that you will be able to use in middle school and throughout the rest of your life!

In this book, you'll have a chance to be your own detective as we investigate what we think is the most interesting part of middle school: the students (that's you!). We will be exploring how **YOUR THOUGHTS** impact **YOUR BEHAVIORS** to help you meet **YOUR GOALS**. We're here to help you feel confident as you tackle these things, take on more responsibility, meet those expectations, learn about yourself, and have some fun along the way!

Are you ready to start this adventure? Let's go!

~ANNA P. & BONNIE M.

INTRODUCTION: GETTING THE LAY OF THE LAND

*I*f you are just starting middle school, you might be wondering (or even worrying) how it's going to go. Or, for those of you that are already in middle school and starting 7th or 8th grade, you might be focusing on how school is getting harder and how you will manage even more expectations. Let's face it, middle school can be scary—but it can also be fun! During middle school, you will have new experiences, face new challenges, and have more independence than you did in elementary school: the school building is bigger, you have a new schedule with classes that are more spread out, you have more teachers, and you have more homework. This can be a lot to adjust to. But keep in mind that there are some good and exciting changes, too! With more choices of classes and interesting clubs, you will have more independence, meet new people, and make new friends.

We want you to think of this book as your roadmap to a new adventure, and us as your tour guides.

YOUR TOUR GUIDES: ANNA AND BONNIE

I'm Anna, and I'm a psychologist working in private practice where I meet with children, teens, and adults to work on goals to take care of their mental health, focusing on issues like stress, anxiety, and feeling good about themselves. Before working in a private practice, I spent a lot of time working in schools, where I helped children and teenagers deal with some of the common challenges that come with being a student.

I'm Bonnie, and I'm a kind of learning specialist called an "educational therapist." I help neurodiverse students who have their own way of thinking that doesn't always match with the strategies used by teachers in school. Many of my students have learning challenges (such as a reading disability or dysgraphia), or trouble regulating their attention and focus and staying organized. My goal is to help make school easier for my students by teaching them strategies to work efficiently and effectively based on how they learn best.

We have known each other for a long time. In fact, we lived in the same town and met when Anna was in middle school! As your tour guides, we will help you get the lay of the land and learn the tools to help you manage the challenges of middle school. We want to show you that you are not alone: all middle schoolers struggle with some aspect of middle school at some point. You'll see some examples of experiences based on actual middle schoolers that we know or were friends with.

MEET THE MAIN STREET CREW
MEET DILLON

Dillon is very active and loves sports and video games! He's lived in the same neighborhood since he was four, but was going to a different school, so this is his first year at Main Street Middle School (MSMS). At his old school, he played soccer, basketball, and baseball, and he can't wait to join those teams at his school this year, too! He usually does pretty well in school... but sometimes he forgets to do his homework.

MEET CARLO

Carlo is the second oldest of five siblings. This is Carlo's second year in middle school. He is creative and loves to draw. His favorite subject in school is art, and his least favorite subject is English. Carlo really wants to get good grades, but it takes him a long time to get his homework done. There is always a lot of fun going on at Carlo's house, but with all those kids it's often noisy, which makes it hard for Carlo to concentrate sometimes.

MEET BRYCE

This is Bryce's first year in middle school. Bryce wants to be involved, and be good at, well...everything! Bryce always has her sights set on the next thing she wants to accomplish, whether it's getting good grades or getting the lead in the school play. When she is not with her friends in the neighborhood, she's at a club meeting, attending band practice or music lessons, volunteering with her community youth group, or studying. She loves being involved, but sometimes finds it hard to make time for everything she wants to do.

MEET MADDIE

Maddie doesn't really like school. She is very quiet in class, and hardly ever raises her hand or volunteers an answer. She is not very interested in math, science, or social studies, and she doesn't really like to read. But Maddie certainly isn't shy! Outside of the classroom, Maddie talks to her friends non-stop and is a true optimist. She loves to be with her friends and is quick to offer encouragement when they are down.

MEET AJ

AJ loves the academic part of school; school just makes sense to them. AJ's parents expect them to bring home straight As, and luckily for AJ, they rarely need to study to get good grades. Outside of academics, AJ isn't as comfortable, and sometimes they have trouble knowing what other people are thinking... which sometimes leads to misunderstandings or makes them angry. If there are more than just a few people around, AJ likes to watch what is going on instead of actually taking part in the activity.

RUMORS YOU MAY HAVE HEARD

Whether you are just starting middle school, getting ready to enter a new grade, or even just starting a new week at school, you probably have ideas in your mind of what your middle school experience will—or should—be like. You might have imagined your perfect day in middle school: one where you are picked class president, make tons of new friends, or are made captain of the soccer team. Or, you might have imagined a day that is more of a disaster: where you can't get your locker open, don't have anywhere to sit in the cafeteria, or trip while walking down the hallway. Maybe you've heard from a friend or an older relative that in middle school the teachers are mean, or you will have

10 hours of homework a night. Whatever rumors you've heard, they're probably a combination of some truth and a healthy dose of exaggeration. Let's talk about some of the rumors (and the truths) that the kids in the crew heard before they started middle school.

RUMOR #1: "You'll never be able to do all the work in middle school!"

The truth: We're not going to lie...the work that you will have to do in middle school is harder than elementary school, but you **can** do it with the right tools. The fact that you're reading this book is a great start! Before you can overcome the academic work challenges of middle school, the first step is for you to start believing that success is possible. If you still aren't convinced, give the kids a chance to show you how they learned to have a positive mindset and believe in themselves.

RUMOR #2: "I have to get straight As. Otherwise it will be a disaster!"

The truth: Many middle school students feel a lot of pressure about grades and friendships—from parents, teachers, friends, and even themselves. Middle school is a time to learn how to become the person you want to be. Working hard and having high expectations is a good thing, but *no one* is perfect—and no one needs to be! If you struggle with that balance, fear not! We will be exploring the tools that the crew each use to create a balance between working toward what they want to accomplish and handling the pressure that comes with it.

RUMOR #3: "In middle school you better do what everyone else does, or no one will like you."

The truth: There are definitely a lot of things that middle school students have in common with each other, but that doesn't mean that you can't be your own person! The kids in the crew are similar in a lot of ways, but they are all unique, too—which is what makes them interesting! You'll probably find that you have something in common with at least one of them, whether it's a preference for how they like to study and learn, activities they like, how they handle stress, or how they manage their schedules. It's OK to do some things the same as your peers *and* to

have characteristics and preferences that make **you**
uniquely, interestingly, wonderfully, **you**!

RUMOR #4: "You'll get lost. You won't be able to open
your locker. You'll never be able to get to class on time.
You won't have enough time to eat lunch."

The truth: Yes, middle school buildings are usually
bigger than elementary school buildings. Yes, in
middle school you'll have more teachers and have to
change classes throughout the day. Yes, opening a
locker can be tricky. But, with the right strategies and
a little practice, you can master all of those things!

WHAT'S IN THIS BOOK

Have you ever gone sightseeing while on a trip with
your family to a new place? You could just start
exploring on your own, but it could be hard to find
your way around and discover the most interesting
tourist attractions if you've never been there before.
It's easier if you have a tour guide who can show
you where to go and what to do so you can make the
most of your adventure. To get an overview of the
highlights, many cities offer tours. The tour guides
take you around the city to talk about the town. You

can stop in various places to spend time looking around, or go on to the next attraction.

We've planned a trip for you that won't be boring, and we've included plenty of interactive activities for you to explore as we go. There is not only one way to sightsee. Some people like to go to every single tourist attraction in order. Some people like to casually roam around the streets a bit more. Some people like to go back to a particular attraction more than once. Just like sightseeing in a new place, we encourage you to use this book in the way that works best for you. We have laid out the chapters in an order that makes sense to us, but if there are particular "attractions" that you are more interested in exploring, go ahead and skip to what interests you. If you want to spend extra time with some of the activities before continuing on, go for it! Whichever way you choose, we are looking forward to sharing this adventure with you.

Our goal is to provide you, a driven, hardworking, eager student, the opportunity to learn some new skills that will help you out not only during middle school, but through all your school years and life in general. We will explore the non-academic parts of middle school success, like mindsets, the power of grit, perseverance, and goal setting, and the impact of pressure. We will also explore the academic skills needed in middle school, like navigating your new environment, dealing with teacher expectations and schedules, and skills for learning information.

We don't expect you to already be an expert at navigating middle school—if you were, there wouldn't be any point in reading this book ☺! But we hope you read this with the goal of learning more about both your strengths and the things you find challenging as you make your way through middle school.

A NOTE FOR THE ADULTS IN YOUR LIFE

You might be just beginning your journey as the parent of a middle schooler, or you might already be deep in the trenches. Either way, you probably have some questions about ways you can help your child navigate the expectations and demands of middle school. You might be thinking, "I already know about middle school. I went to middle school." But the reality is that it's much different now than it used to be. Not only in terms of what is taught but *how* it's taught, the use and impact of technology, frequency of communication with teachers, classroom expectations, and increased demand for organization. Learning these things takes time and effort, and middle school can be a stressful time for kids; they are not just being "dramatic." We hope the information in this book helps your child learn more about themself and provides you with an opportunity to explore alongside them.

This book will teach your child how to adopt the best approaches to their thinking (mindset, grit, and motivation) and specific strategies for school success (navigating the environment, learning styles and study strategies, executive functioning, and stress management). Within each chapter, your child will have opportunities to "be their own detective" to learn more about themselves and how they approach problems using cognitive and behavioral concepts that incorporate thoughts, feelings, and behaviors. To help your child be actively involved in the material of this book, we have included interactive activities, such as fun quizzes, so they can learn more about themselves and implement tools and strategies to help them achieve their goals. We strongly encourage you to talk with your child about the activities with an open mind and a positive attitude! Even if you find that your child is not yet where you want them to be, keep in mind that this is a time of exploration and growth. We hope this book serves as the first step in building self-awareness as a middle school student.

As a parent, middle school is a time when you might want to practice stepping back a bit, allowing your child to figure it out and even fail at times. Doing this now, even if it involves letting them learn from their mistakes, is the right time since the stakes are lower than they will be in high school. We know that parent involvement is related to school success, so by no means are we suggesting you be uninvolved; rather, the idea is that stepping back at times will create more independence and will likely foster feelings of ownership and accountability for their work. So this is the time to encourage them to be curious, creative, and figure out their best approach to school and learning. For example, when your child wants to try a new strategy, give them a chance for a trial run, and then afterwards, help them assess if it worked for them or if it needs to be tweaked. Amongst the many parenting goals during the middle school years, you want to help your child develop intrinsic (internal) motivation and become more invested in their learning process and academic growth. One way to support this is to encourage your child to generate their own ideas, solve problems on their own, and advocate for themselves. It will be a gradual process for sure, but you want to find the right balance of being there to help them while also supporting their independence.

Middle school is often a time when learning challenges and differences become apparent. Some kids breeze through elementary school only to discover in 6th or 7th grade that they struggle to focus or stay organized. Or that reading and comprehending doesn't come as easily as it did in the past. As the work becomes more sophisticated, and as they have more to manage and be responsible for, certain learning challenges such as attention-deficit/hyperactivity disorder (ADHD), a reading disability (such as dyslexia), and others may become apparent. If you are concerned, we recommend talking with your school counselor, pediatrician, or if possible, a reputable psychologist for possible educational and/or neuropsychological testing. While getting a diagnosis can be emotional, having a clear understanding of your child's strengths and challenges and how they can use their strengths to support their challenges now—before high school—is essential. Moreover, it can help protect your child's self-esteem to know, for example, that they have inattentive-type ADHD and it's not that they aren't motivated or trying hard enough. Then they can explore options for interventions and supports and feel relieved that there are good resources out there to help.

We know you want what is best for your child, and sometimes their output doesn't align with your expectations. Many caregivers of middle school kids can sometimes judge their child's work to be less than excellent, or inadvertently compare their child to their siblings or peers. It's important to avoid comparisons and labels such as "lazy," "unmotivated," or "uncaring." Remember that it's your voice that's often in your child's head when they are struggling, and we want that voice to be one of support, encouragement, and positivity. We encourage you to show your child that you believe in them, are there for them, and understand that managing this transition to middle school—both the academic and social aspects—is not easy. Feeling understood and supported by you, their caregiver, is one of the best protective factors you can offer them for their mental health and well-being.

~ANNA P. AND BONNIE M.

Chapter 1

Mindsets Matter

Our first stop is to learn about the importance of your mindset when it comes to school. A mindset is basically your general attitude about things—how you tend to think about situations and tasks, and how you react to the world. Let's take a look at how each of the crew reacted to getting a math test back.

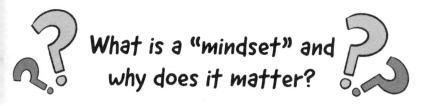

What is a "mindset" and why does it matter?

Each kid reacted differently to the same situation. When they got their test back, both AJ and Bryce felt confident that they had been well-prepared and thought they probably did well. Dillon and Carlo did not expect to do well, and Maddie had no idea how she did. Their reactions were based on how they felt and thought about their own abilities, skills, and talents.

I'm sure you've heard people say that no one is good at everything, and it's really true! Everyone has a different set of skills that they're good at, and some skills that they're not so good at. Being good at something might start as a natural ability that you seem to be born with, but mostly it requires practice. When something comes easily, it's natural to want to do it more often because it's fun! But when things don't come easily, many people give up. It's easy to see why they wouldn't want to keep working at it.

NOT GIVING UP, AND INSTEAD WORKING ON IT UNTIL YOU FIGURE IT OUT OR GET GOOD AT IT, IS CALLED "PERSISTENCE" OR "GRIT." WE'LL TALK MORE ABOUT THAT IN THE NEXT CHAPTER.

It all starts with your belief system: you need to believe in yourself. When someone believes that they can learn new things, they are more willing to face challenges and try hard. The open-minded belief that everyone has the potential to learn and grow is called a **growth mindset.** A growth mindset is based on knowing that skills and abilities can change over time, and you can improve from where you currently are. With practice and effort, you can become more skilled, smarter, and more talented at something. On the other hand, when someone doesn't believe that they have the potential to do well and learn new things, and that their skill level or intelligence is unchangeable, it's called a **fixed mindset.** When someone has a fixed mindset, they often give up on things that don't come easily, and don't put in the effort or time that is needed for them to do well. Sometimes they might even decide not to try at all because they don't want to fail or look "stupid" in front of other people.

A GROWTH MINDSET IS WHEN YOU BELIEVE THAT WITH EFFORT YOUR SKILLS AND ABILITIES CAN CHANGE OVER TIME.

Why does mindset matter, and what does it have to do with middle school? Well, people with a growth mindset actually can, and do, improve their skills. People with a fixed mindset stay stuck in place. People with a growth mindset are more willing to take chances, experience new things, find creative ways to overcome obstacles—and make some mistakes along the way—without giving up. Those are the things that help you reach your goals in middle school and beyond! A fixed mindset limits you and leaves you stuck where you are, and you miss the chance to learn to work through obstacles, which is part of becoming resilient.

Everyone is different. It's possible to have a growth mindset sometimes and a fixed mindset other times. Just like there are probably times when you feel confident and self-assured, and times you are filled with self-doubt. That's perfectly normal, and that's our mindset at work! People don't just have a "growth mindset" or a "fixed mindset" all the time... mindsets are actually on a continuum, meaning that there may be some situations where you have more of a growth mindset (which leads you to feel confident, valued, strong, and happy) and some situations where you have more of a fixed mindset (leading you to feel frustrated, unimportant, weak, or upset).

 What is your mindset?

 Quiz

LET'S FIGURE OUT WHERE YOUR MINDSET FALLS ON THE PATH FROM FIXED TO GROWTH.

On the next pages are some thoughts and reactions that real middle school students have had. Which of the reactions is closest to how you think you would react? They might not exactly match what you would think, of course, but try to choose which one seems closest. Grab a piece of paper and keep track of your answers.

SITUATION:	I MIGHT THINK SOMETHING LIKE:	
Your teacher, Mr. Jones, just returned yesterday's homework and in red marker at the top of the page is "SEE ME!"	**A:** Mr. Jones hates me! Homework is stupid and pointless!	**B:** Uh, oh...I must not have done very well on last night's homework assignment. Maybe I can ask Mr. Jones what I did wrong and fix my mistakes so that I can get extra points.
Your math teacher explained how to solve equations today, but you are still very confused.	**A:** I am SO bad at math. Why even bother trying? It will never make sense and I will never use it! Why do they teach us this stupid stuff?	**B:** Math is not my favorite subject, but I know it will help me in the future, and it's a big part of school. How can I think about that math problem in a way that connects it to something that I care about?
You didn't have time to finish the reading assignment that was due today, and your teacher had you come to her at lunch to finish it.	**A:** My teacher thinks that I'm lazy and that's why I didn't read the chapter she assigned this week.	**B:** There was a reason that I'm behind on the reading assignment. Maybe if I tell my teacher why I wasn't able to finish it, she'll be able to help me get caught up with the rest of the class.
At today's assembly, your friend Jenny was given another award. This was the third one she got this month, but you've never gotten even one.	**A:** Jenny gets good grades and the "best student" awards because she is a teacher's pet. My teachers hate me, so I will never get those things the way Jenny does.	**B:** All the teachers do like Jenny. They make a big deal out of everything she does. It's hard not to get any awards while she gets so many, but I bet if I keep trying, I will get an award for something.
Yesterday's science test was returned today, and you got a 60%.	**A:** I failed the science test. I am stupid.	**B:** I don't understand the information on that science test...yet. I may have failed this time, but I can learn science! It's just a matter of finding the right approach for me and taking the time I need to practice the information.

Your English teacher makes the class take turns answering questions and reading aloud in class, which you hate!	**A:** People will think I'm dumb if I don't have the right answer or if I make mistakes when I read out loud.	**B:** I get nervous when I have to read aloud in class. If I tell my teacher why I don't like it, maybe she'll agree to only call on me when I've raised my hand.
Your essays were returned today, and there are a lot of changes that your teacher wants you to make. There were red marks all over your paper.	**A:** My teacher gave me a bad grade on my essay draft. Why even bother to make the revisions she suggested? I'm a terrible writer.	**B:** OK, my grade on that draft wasn't as good as I had hoped. My mom told me that even professional writers get feedback from their editors. If I ask my teacher for help and make the changes she suggests, I think that I can get a better grade on the next draft.
You have to learn how to read the periodic table, but you're really struggling.	**A:** Why even try? I'm just not smart enough to do this science!	**B:** I am struggling to learn how to read the periodic table. I think I should try a different strategy, like color-coding it to help myself understand how it all fits together.
You have to do a fitness test in PE today.	**A:** I can't run a mile! I'll just skip PE class today so I don't have to participate.	**B:** Running is not something I enjoy or am used to, and it's hard! I might not be able to run the whole time yet, but I can run until I get tired, and then walk until I catch my breath. Even if it takes me a long time or I walk most of the way, I will get to the end of that mile!
A project was due today and you didn't start it until last night, so you ran out of time and just threw something together at the last minute.	**A:** That project was way too long. Mr. Kitts never should have made us do all of that work. It's not fair!	**B:** I didn't do as well as I thought I would on that project. I didn't think it would take much time, so I waited until the night before it was due to start it. Next time, I'll plan to start earlier so that I have enough time to finish everything.

Count up your As and Bs. Which do you have more of?

Everything in the A column is an example of a fixed mindset, and everything in the B column is a growth mindset. If you had more As, that's okay! The whole point of learning about this is so you can learn how to develop a growth mindset—and there's is no time like the present to start. If you chose more B answers, you're off to a great start to having a growth mindset...but don't stop now—there's always room for growth!

Here are some of the main pieces of developing a growth mindset:

- **SELF-EFFICACY** is the belief that you can do something. This doesn't mean showing proof that you did something; it means believing in yourself that you have the ability. Like how AJ believed they would do well on their math test.

- **LOCUS OF CONTROL** is where you believe the control in a situation lies—either within your control or outside of it. If you feel like you can impact a situation or how it turns out, that's an *internal* locus of control. If you feel like you can't change a situation or how it turns out, that's an *external* locus of control. For example, Bryce had an internal locus of control when she felt that she would be able to get her assignment done on time because she felt in control of the steps in the assignment. On the other hand, when Dillon finished the assignment, he was relieved and said, "wow, that was really lucky," which was an example of an external locus of control. He thought it was all luck and not something that came from his efforts.

- **PERSONAL AGENCY** is being an agent of change in your own life—meaning that you have the sense that you can take control and make things happen. It involves self-efficacy, internal locus of control, and skill; it's about believing that you can do it and knowing what it takes to get it done (developing the skills needed). It's both knowing what steps you need to take, and the ability to keep trying until you finish.

How do self-efficacy, locus of control, and personal agency relate to having a growth mindset?

Great question! To reach your goals, first, you have to **believe you can** do something (self-efficacy), then you need to **believe you have control** over the outcome (internal locus of control). Then you have to **act on those beliefs** by putting forth the effort to make those beliefs become a reality (personal agency).

IT ALL COMES DOWN TO BELIEVING IN YOURSELF AND LEARNING THE NECESSARY SKILLS.

These concepts are helpful to know, not just for middle school, but for your whole life! We will discuss them in more detail in upcoming chapters. (If any of these terms are still a little tricky to understand, don't worry, you'll see more examples as we go!)

Take a Minute!

- There are some situations where each of us already has a positive outlook (a growth mindset) about how things will turn out. And there are some times where we think we know exactly what the outcome will be before we even begin (a fixed mindset). The first step in moving along the continuum towards a more growth mindset is recognizing when you have a fixed mindset. Think about these questions:

- Is there a particular teacher or coach who is always on your side, who motivates you to keep trying?

- Do you think that you are athletic, so you will probably be able to learn a new sport easily?

- Do you love the challenge of solving math puzzles?

- Are there different strategies that you use when studying?

- Do you always use the same study or organizational method (even if it doesn't work well for you)?

- Do you feel like it is pointless to learn a new skill unless you can master it?

- Is there a particular class that you think you might fail because the teacher doesn't like you?

- Do you think that math or science will just always be hard for you to understand?

The first four questions show a growth mindset, while the last four show a fixed mindset. Knowing what a growth mindset looks like will help you recognize where you are on the mindset continuum.

Grab a pen! ✏️

We all have a mixture of growth and fixed mindsets. Think about some events, situations, or people in your life that encourage you to have a growth mindset. Then, think about some events, situations, or people in your life that jump-start your fixed mindset (hint: these might be things you avoid or dread). Grab a piece of paper and write down three of each.

Our mindsets are based on how we think, so it's important to take some time to pay attention to our thoughts. Do you find yourself thinking with a fixed mindset? Do you find yourself thinking you *can't* or *won't* be able to do something before you've even started? People have thousands of thoughts every day and often don't even realize when they're happening. Many of our thoughts are automatic thoughts, which are just what they sound like: thoughts that "pop up" or seem to happen automatically without any prompting. Some thoughts encourage us, but others are not so helpful. When our thoughts are not helpful, or are even hurtful, they are labeled as "negative thinking." When your thoughts are directed toward yourself, and they are negative, that is called "negative self-talk." Some examples of negative self-talk are: "I'm so stupid," "I can't do this," or "Everyone else is better at this than me."

AN AUTOMATIC THOUGHT IS A THOUGHT THAT JUST POPS UP WITHOUT ANY EFFORT.

The tricky part is that we don't always realize when we're doing it! Do you notice that some or many of your thoughts are negative and activate your fixed mindset? Have you ever caught yourself saying negative self-talk over and over (and over) in your mind? This is "stewing" in your thoughts, and stewing in negative thoughts is not what you want to do! When this happens, obviously the goal is to stop the negative thoughts. But you have to recognize when you're having negative thoughts before you can stop them! It's also important to consider how the thoughts influence our feelings and behavior.

Let's look at what happened to Carlo while he was working on a self-portrait. As he was drawing, he began to think it looked nothing like him, and that he was never going to be able to get it right. Carlo started to draw more and more aggressively, and he accidentally poked the pencil through the paper. Immediately, Carlo ripped his paper up and threw it in the trash.

Clearly, Carlo had a fixed mindset about drawing his self-portrait. But he—and you!—can learn to recognize his negative thoughts and develop a growth mindset with some simple tools.

GROWTH MINDSET TOOLBOX

Cognitive-behavioral therapy (CBT) helps teach strategies to manage stress, anxiety, and even a low mood. CBT investigates the thoughts, feelings, and behaviors we have in response to a situation, and looks at how we can improve all three. These growth-mindset-building tools are all based in CBT.

TOOL #1 THOUGHTS–FEELINGS–BEHAVIOR LOG

Separating out your thoughts and feelings from your actions helps you change your perspective and recognize when you are thinking with a fixed mindset. First, think of a situation where you were frustrated with a school assignment, homework, or project. Then, grab a pen and piece of paper and make four columns titled "situation," "thought," "feeling," and "behavior." Try answering these question prompts if you need some help getting started. It's usually easiest to start with writing about the situation, but you don't have to fill in each column in order—do whatever works for you!

Check out Carlo's thought log as an example. Carlo was able to recognize that his automatic thoughts led to feeling frustrated and influenced his exaggerated belief that he would never be successful.

SITUATION:	THOUGHT:	FEELING:	BEHAVIOR:
working on an art assignment self-portrait	"This drawing stinks. I will never get it to look like me. I will never be able to do this."	angry defeated frustrated	tore up and threw away my drawing

Becoming aware of your thoughts can allow you to use them to your advantage. With the next few tools, you'll learn how to change these automatic thoughts—and *changing the way you think will change the way you feel!*

TOOL #2: POSITIVE SELF-TALK

Positive self-talk is also exactly what it sounds like: talking to yourself in a positive way! Positive self-talk can be used to pump yourself up, build confidence, and make you feel better about yourself. Research has found that positive thoughts improve mood, increase self-esteem, help with stress, and provide support during challenging experiences. You can also use it to fight back against the negative self-talk or automatic thoughts you may find yourself thinking. Sometimes we are not as kind to ourselves as we are to other people. It can be helpful to ask yourself, "if my friend had this thought, what would I say to them?" or "What would someone who loves me say in response to my thought?" Just like any habit, the more you practice positive self-talk, the more natural and automatic it will become. Even if at first the thoughts don't feel true, try using them anyway—you'd be surprised at how helpful they can still be! And eventually they will start to feel real. Check out the examples of positive self-talk on the next page. We recommend you write these down on note cards, and create more of your own.

"I am worthy."

"I can do this!"

"I am strong."

"I work really hard."

"I love myself and need to support myself."

"I won't give up!"

"I can do so much when I put my mind to it!"

"I can try my best."

"I trust myself."

"I will stick with this."

"I'm uncomfortable and I can handle it."

"I am proud of myself for trying."

"I'm in charge of myself."

"I believe in myself."

"Today is going to be a good day!"

"Just because I don't feel good right now doesn't mean I won't feel better later."

"Fear is only a feeling. It cannot hold me back."

TOOL #3 REFRAMING THOUGHTS

It's important to try to see a negative situation as not all negative. Have you ever heard your friends, family, or teachers say, "try to be positive," or "think optimistically"? This is also known as "reframing your thoughts," and it encourages you to see a situation from a different perspective. You could also see it as fighting back against the negative self-talk.

For example, last week, Maddie struggled with a writing assignment and ended up earning a lower grade than she wanted. A negative way to view this situation would be if Maddie had said, "I can never do this right. I always fail" (which could also be considered a fixed mindset). On the other hand, by reframing her thoughts about the situation, Maddie could think, "This experience taught me that I need to plan more time to organize and write the paper. Learning how to do things differently and better is what being a student is all about."

REFRAMING THOUGHTS IS A VERY IMPORTANT SKILL, AND IT CAN TAKE TIME TO PRACTICE.

Original thought: "There is no way I'm trying out for the travel baseball team. I'm not good enough."

Reframed thought: "The more I practice and stay motivated, the more prepared I will be."

Original thought: "She must be mad at me because she didn't text me back."

Reframed thought: "Maybe she's busy with her family or hasn't read my message yet."

Original thought: "I really messed up on my first English paper."

Reframed thought: "It's not realistic to be perfect and get a 100% every time."

Original thought: "I'm never going to like school."

Reframed thought: "If I stay open-minded, I might learn about something that interests me."

Original thought: "I can't ever come up with a creative project."

Reframed thought: "I've gotten compliments for my creativity before. I'm just stuck right now."

One way to reframe your thoughts is by adding a very small word that can make a lot of difference. Adding this word will allow you to think about a situation with less trepidation, worry, or fear. The word is "yet." By adding the word "yet" to the end of a thought, you are reminding yourself that even though you can't do something right now, you *can* learn how to do it in the future! It's just not the future...yet ☺.

Grab a pen! ✏️

Let's think again about Maddie's situation...instead of her thinking, "I'll never be able to do this," she could think, "I can't do this, *yet*." Now you give it a try. On a sheet of notebook paper, write three to five statements that you can't do (but you might like to!). Then go back and add the word "yet" at the end of each. Adding "yet" makes you feel more optimistic, doesn't it?

Take a look back at the growth mindset statements on pages 34-35. Notice anything? The thoughts and reactions in column B were examples of growth mindsets that use the tools we just talked about: believing in yourself, reframing your thoughts, positive self-talk, and using the word "yet." Moving from a fixed mindset to a growth mindset takes practice, but we promise it's worth the time and effort that it takes! With practice, it will become automatic for you to think this way.

MOVING FROM A FIXED MINDSET TO A GROWTH MINDSET TAKES PRACTICE, BUT IT'S WORTH IT!

PRACTICE, PRACTICE, PRACTICE

Try out these activities to practice growing your growth mindset:

- *Make a three-column list.* In the first column, list some things you cannot control (like the weather, other people's actions, or your age). In the second column, list some things you can control (like what you have for a snack, your tone of voice, or who your friends are). In the third column, list some things you don't have control of *yet*, but will be able to in the future (like being well-prepared for your Spanish test, or taking good photographs). Writing it all out like this is a great way to get yourself to recognize and focus on the things you can (or will be able to) actually control, and not waste your energy worrying about the things you can't.

- *Move toward a growth mindset.* Make ten growth-mindset statements and put each on a sticky note or note card (like: "use 'yet' self-talk," "learn from a past mistake," "reframe my thoughts," etc.). Put them all on one side of your bathroom mirror or the wall of your bedroom. Each day, try to use one of those growth-mindset statements and move that sticky note to the other side of the mirror or wall when you've done it. Celebrate your growth mindset when you've completed all 10!

- *Act out your mindset.* Act out two scenarios for the same situation, first with a fixed mindset and then another scene for the same situation where the mindset is a growth mindset. What were the differences?

- *Design a comic strip.* Write a comic strip or a story that shows a situation where a character encounters a problem and gets through it by using a growth mindset.

This chapter had a lot of information! We reviewed mindsets, self-efficacy, locus of control, personal agency, positive self-talk, and how to reframe your thoughts. Now that you have a better idea what kind of mindset you have, you can start to approach situations with more flexibility and openness to challenges, which will help you accomplish your goals. In the next chapter, we will be talking about grit and goal setting. See you there!

Chapter 2

Grit: The Power of Perseverance

Welcome to Chapter 2! This is may be one of the most important chapters to help you navigate your way through middle school successfully. You will learn about grit and why it's so essential.

Main Street Middle School is having a perseverance awareness week. Each student is supposed to research a famous person who worked really hard and stuck with their goals even when it was tough.

- Dillon chose **MICHAEL JORDAN**. From the time Michael was a little kid he wanted to go to college and be a professional athlete. At first, he didn't think he would achieve his goal, because he was cut from his high school basketball team. But he eventually became an NBA star!

- Maddie chose **BETHANY HAMILTON**. Bethany had a dream of being a professional surfer. She lost her left arm in a shark attack but still went on to become a nationally ranked surfer.

- Bryce chose **HARRIET TUBMAN**. Harriet helped rescue dozens of enslaved people, despite putting herself in danger every trip she took.

- AJ chose **ALBERT EINSTEIN**. Even though Einstein was one of the most intelligent and influential men ever, he failed his college entrance exams the first time he took them.

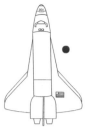

- Carlo chose **RICHARD BRANSON**. Richard has a learning disability and dropped out of school when he was 15 years old. As an adult, he started Virgin Records, an airline, and even a spacecraft company (he was one of the first people to go into outer space on his own rocket)!

AJ, Carlo, Maddie, Bryce, and Dillon all chose different famous people who were amazing examples of people who persevered. Even though they each faced significant obstacles on the path to reaching their goals, they kept going, even when it got hard. The perseverance, passion, and effort they put forth to complete their goals is called *"grit."*

What is Grit?

Grit is not just for famous people—it's for everyone! And now is the perfect time to practice grit, because the demands of middle school require determination and perseverance.

IT TAKES GRIT TO ACCOMPLISH MORE COMPLEX TASKS AND ASSIGNMENTS.

Before middle school, your job as a student was to learn specific skills, like reading, writing, and memorizing math facts. Now that you are in middle school, your job is to take those skills and apply them to more challenging tasks, like writing essays and solving algebra problems.

Bryce had grit when she was completing a long-term social studies project that required several weeks of reading her textbook, looking up articles on the internet, asking her teacher questions, and creating her final project. Dillon needs grit right now to complete a study guide that he'll review with his teacher during lunch for a couple weeks to bump up his science grade.

GRIT IS WHAT HELPS YOU PUSH THROUGH CHALLENGING TASKS!

Quiz

UNDERSTANDING YOUR GRIT LEVEL

This quiz will give you a quick estimate of your level of grit. Grab a piece of paper and a pen. Read each statement and give yourself one, two, or three points for each grit characteristic statement.

	RARELY	SOMETIMES	OFTEN
1. I have goals for my future that I am excited about and believe I can accomplish.	1	2	3
2. When I play sports or an instrument, I practice a lot so that I can get better.	1	2	3
3. When a friend or someone in my family asks me to do something, I do it (even when there are other things I would rather be doing).	1	2	3
4. When I get a bad grade on a test, I try to find a different way to study for the next time.	1	2	3
5. When I lose at a game, I try to figure out a better strategy to use the next time.	1	2	3
6. When I have an important assignment to do for school, I do not get distracted by fun things.	1	2	3
7. When I'm struggling with a hard assignment, I ask for help and keep trying until I get it.	1	2	3
8. When I join a club or do a group project, I follow through on my responsibilities even if others don't.	1	2	3
9. When there is something that I really want but I don't have enough money for it yet, I can wait patiently until I have enough money saved up to get it.	1	2	3
10. I have a "don't give up" attitude.	1	2	3
11. When something is hard, I usually stick with it until I figure it out.	1	2	3
12. I can keep doing things that I am not interested in.	1	2	3

Now, add up your total points to see how much grit
you have.

If you had **28-36 points**, you already have a lot of grit,
perseverance, and stick-with-it-ness.

If you had **20-27 points**, you are on the way to being a
"gritty" person.

If you had **12-19 points**, while there are some times where
you show grit, there are other times where you have more
trouble pushing through in the face of challenges.

Regardless of your grit score, don't stop being
"gritty" now! The activities and tools in the rest
of this chapter will help you acquire more grit. If
you learned from the quiz above that you do not
have a lot of grit, remember to tap into your growth
mindset and say,

*I don't have a lot of grit—**yet!***

HOW TO BECOME "GRITTIER"

Did you know that there has been a lot of research about what makes people successful in life? When researchers study success, what they consistently find is surprising to many people, and it might surprise you, too. **THE BOTTOM LINE IS: THE BIGGEST FACTOR THAT PREDICTS SUCCESS IS NOT ACTUALLY INTELLIGENCE OR TALENT, IT'S GRIT.**

A high level of grit is a better predictor of success in all areas, not just academics: sports, art, music, and careers are all improved when you have grit. Those with a strong work ethic and "stick-with-it-ness" who don't give up in the face of obstacles and bumps in the road are the most successful.

HAVE YOU EVER HEARD THE STORY OF "THE LITTLE ENGINE THAT COULD?" It's a well-known story because the moral is so valuable. That little engine desperately wanted to pull a heavy load up a hill, but the enginge was small, the load was heavy, and the outlook seemed bleak. The little engine decided to give it a try anyway, even in the face of self-doubt, repeating the mantra "I think I can, I think I can," as it inched its way up the hill—and reached its goal of making it over!

Some people are naturally "gritty" people. You can probably imagine someone you know who works extremely hard, pushes through challenging tasks, and never seems to give up (like the little engine). Maybe it's a parent, guardian, sibling, friend, teacher, or someone else you know. These people can be great models for you to watch as they persist through challenging situations!

But most people need to build grit and learn how to stick with tasks that aren't easy or fun. You can do this by **MAKING A PLAN TO PRACTICE BEING GRITTY, ENCOURAGING YOURSELF ALONG THE WAY, AND CELEBRATING YOUR ACCOMPLISHMENT** when you do complete the goal.

Speaking of practice, the *way* you practice matters. Research on grit emphasizes the importance of **DELIBERATE, MINDFUL PRACTICE**. Deliberate practice is the purposeful and organized effort that you put in as you work towards a goal. When you don't think mindfully about your intent, practice can involve mindless repetition, leading to a lot of time spent with not a lot of progress to show for it. We will talk more about deliberate practice in Chapter 6.

So, what do you do when the thing you are supposed to practice is something you find boring?

People want to spend more time on things they find interesting and less time on things they don't enjoy—of course! That means sometimes you need to find a way to motivate yourself, even when you aren't interested. It can be hard to find, but there is usually something in that task that sparks your interest (at least a little bit). For example, when Maddie was working on her history project, she discovered a new presentation method using a comic strip creator online that she really enjoyed and is excited about using again.

If you're not sure what interests you, middle school is a great time to start investigating. Tap into your growth mindset and encourage yourself to explore! Experience and exposure will help you find what you are interested in—and what you are not, which is just as important.

YOU'RE NOT GOING TO LOVE EVERYTHING YOU HAVE TO DO IN MIDDLE SCHOOL—NO ONE LOVES EVERYTHING THEY HAVE TO DO ALL THE TIME! THIS IS WHEN YOU CAN RELY ON YOUR GRIT TO SEE YOU THROUGH.

GIVING YOURSELF A ROADMAP

People often say that they will "work harder" or "try harder" to reach their goals. For example, if the goal is to get on the basketball team, they might say that they need to "try harder to make it." The desire to work or try "harder" to achieve your goals is a great start...but what does "harder" actually mean? To reach your goal, you need to have a detailed roadmap.

THERE IS A FAMOUS QUOTE FROM THE BOOK *THE LITTLE PRINCE: A GOAL WITHOUT A PLAN IS JUST A WISH.*

Setting clear and specific goals is important. It helps you understand exactly what you want, focus your thoughts and actions, and increase your chance of succeeding, all while using your time wisely. Planning the steps out and thinking about what obstacles you might face actually saves you time in the long run! It's like the difference between using GPS (or a map) and just wandering around. You might eventually get where you want to go without planning out your trip, but you'll probably make some wrong turns on the way, and it will take you a lot longer.

Sometimes people seem to automatically know what to do to reach their goals, but most of the time, people need to use tools to help them. Check out how Bryce, Dillon, and Carlo completed their school projects.

- Bryce seemed to intuitively know all of the small steps she needed to take to tackle the project. She dove right in and started her research and brainstorming project ideas.

- Thinking about the entire project all at once was overwhelming for Dillon, so he used strategies to separate out the smaller steps. He made an outline of the information he wanted to research, created a list of the materials he would need, and made a plan to practice presenting it.

- Carlo needed to create an even more clear, detailed plan for himself to help him break down the project into even smaller parts so that he could do just a little bit at a time. So he set aside a specific amount of time each day to do one small part. The first day, he brainstormed topics, the next day he found sources about his topic, the next few days he took notes using a graphic organizer. Then he worked on the final product in chunks each day to spread out the work.

We'll talk about some actual tools to grow grit in a second, but first, take a look at these ideas for ways to use grit and deliberate practice to set and reach goals. Do any of these sound like something you could do?

- Dillon set a goal to learn all of the prime numbers between one and 100 by heart. He chunked them into groups of three numbers (like 2-3-5) and repeated the chunks aloud several times each day. Once he knew a set of three by heart, he added on another set of three numbers. He practiced them for a few minutes every day for three weeks, and now knows them by heart.

- Maddie set a goal to learn a new cheerleading routine, but had a hard time remembering the order of the steps. She broke down the routine into smaller sections, and practiced each one twice a day until she had that part memorized, then added the next section into her daily practice. After one month, she finally had it memorized and was ready for tryouts.

- AJ set a goal to speak up more in class. Each day they try to raise their hand at least once when the teacher asks a question. By the end of the month, their teacher pulled them aside and told them how much she appreciates their class participation.

SETTING GOALS FOR YOURSELF HELPS TO CLARIFY YOUR INTENT, FOCUS YOUR THOUGHTS AND ACTIONS, AND INCREASE YOUR CHANCES OF SUCCESS.

It's also important that you plan for potential obstacles; when you are working toward a goal, it won't always go smoothly. Sometimes you might realize that you don't have all the materials you need, you may not understand a part of the assignment, or you may get caught up in a negative automatic thought (remember those from the last chapter?).

Here are some fairly common obstacles and possible solutions that you might encounter in middle school:

- If you forgot to write down your homework assignment, you can call a friend in your class.

- If you have trouble remembering your math facts, you can use a calculator while you do your homework.

- If you do not understand the directions, you can ask your teacher for help.

- If you feel discouraged and want to give up, you can give yourself a pep talk.

- If you often forget to bring your lunch to school, you can leave yourself a note by the front door.

Take a Minute!

Can you think of any other obstacles that are common for you? The goal is to expect there might be bumps, so you don't get tripped up on them and can just problem-solve and move forward.

REALITY CHECK! You may not know how to set a specific goal, or you may have a hard time deciding what your goal should even be, so it might be useful to ask a parent or teacher. Also, some goals are *long-term* (like a marathon), and others are *short-term* (like a sprint), and goals vary in importance and level of difficulty. It's important to think about all these things when you're creating a goal!

GOAL-SETTING AND GRIT TOOLBOX

If you can think of a time you set a goal and then persevered through a challenge to reach that goal, then you have already started building your grit. Growing grit takes deliberate practice, but with the right tools, you can do it!

TOOL #1: MIND MAPS

Mind Maps are helpful when there are a lot of possible ways to reach your goal. The goal of the mind map is to see your thoughts in another form—visually—and make them more specific. Mind maps are a way to break down big tasks into smaller chunks so that you can focus on one small piece at a time. Look at the mind map that Dillon created when he was trying to make the basketball team.

Dillon's Mind Map

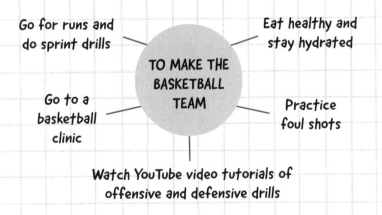

Go for runs and do sprint drills

Eat healthy and stay hydrated

TO MAKE THE BASKETBALL TEAM

Go to a basketball clinic

Practice foul shots

Watch YouTube video tutorials of offensive and defensive drills

These smaller goals are all things that will definitely help Dillon improve his basketball performance—and they're a lot more helpful than Dillon just deciding to "try harder," aren't they?

A mind map has a central goal in the middle with lines radiating outward with small steps you want to take to reach that goal. To make your own mind map:

1. Identify your goal.

2. Write it in the center of a blank piece of paper and draw a circle around it.

3. Think about tasks that will help you reach your goal and write them around the circle.

4. Allow your thoughts to flow, and don't worry about any particular order. Write as many small tasks as you can think of—they don't all have to be realistic right now! Just get the thoughts down.

5. Now decide on which of the ideas sound like good starting points, circle them, and connect them to your goal. Then get started! ☺

TOOL #2: GOAL STAIRCASE

Goal Staircases are helpful when you have a lot of smaller steps that build on each other to lead up to an ultimate goal. Think about when you're walking up a staircase. You have to start at the bottom and work your way up to the top, one step at a time.

Check out the Goal Staircase that AJ created when they were working on the history project.

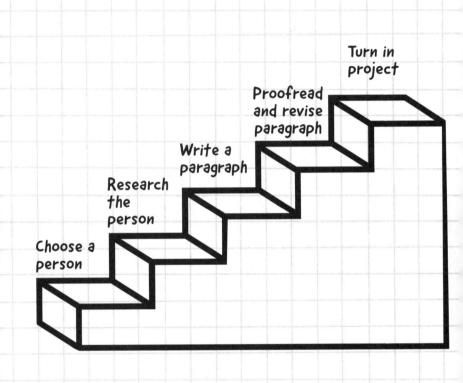

Turn in project

Proofread and revise paragraph

Write a paragraph

Research the person

Choose a person

Grab a pen! ✒️

TRY A GOAL STAIRCASE FOR YOURSELF!

1. Sketch a staircase like AJ's on a piece of paper.

2. Think of a fairly large goal you'd like to accomplish and write it on the top step.

3. Think of the smaller goals that you have to reach first to get to that bigger goal, and write those smaller goals on the steps, in the order they need to be done.

4. Start on the first step and work your way up until you're done!

TOOL #3 "FIRST–THEN" STRATEGY

It's easier to stick with a task when you feel invested in it! That's why practicing your favorite sport or hobby probably doesn't usually feel like a chore. But sometimes we have to do things we aren't very interested in or excited about. To get yourself invested, try rewarding yourself! The reward should be something that pumps you up (like taking a short break, using technology, playing a sport, having a small treat, or something a little more special like going to see a movie or getting your favorite dinner). The reward should match the size of the task. It's not realistic to buy a new video game after reading one chapter for English class, but it is reasonable to take a 10-minute break to play a video game.

A great way to make a reward plan is with the First-Then strategy. *First,* identify the things you need to get done, *then* decide what you will reward yourself with after completing the task. Here are a few examples from the crew:

	FIRST	THEN
MADDIE	First, I complete my math homework.	Then I get to watch one episode of my favorite TV show.
CARLO	First, I finishing cleaning my room.	Then I get to draw in my sketchbook.
DILLON	First, I read one section of my history book.	Then I get to play basketball with my friends.
BRYCE	First, I make half of my flash cards for a science test.	Then I get to look at my phone for 10 minutes.
AJ	First, I make the honor roll.	Then I get to choose where we go out for dinner to celebrate.

Grab a pen!

What are some things that would be good rewards for you? Try making a chart like the crew's with some things you need to get done, and some rewards to go along with them!

Now you know about the power of grit, how to become gritter, and how to make a plan for your goals. In the next chapter, we will tackle the pressures of middle school!

Chapter 3

The Pitfalls of Pressure and Mastering Motivation

$\mathcal{W}$elcome to Chapter 3! We know there is nothing fun about pressure, but it's important to understand what pressure is in order to spend more time with motivation instead! In this chapter, we're going to talk about the difference between motivation and pressure (they're not the same!). First, story time:

About 80 years ago, a **FAMOUS SCHOLAR NAMED HARRY HARLOW** studied monkeys to find out how they learn. He had the monkeys complete simple puzzles that involved pulling out a pin, undoing a hook, and lifting a cover. Harlow and his team expected this task would be more challenging for the monkeys than it was for humans, and that they would need to teach them how to do it and give an incentive to motivate the monkeys. But what they found was surprising: without any direction or prompting, the monkeys independently began to work on the puzzles and kept at it until they solved them! In fact, the monkeys were determined and seemed to enjoy the process of figuring out how to solve the puzzles. **THE MONKEYS DID NOT NEED REWARDS OR EVEN PRAISE FOR COMPLETING THE PUZZLES** correctly. These observations left the investigators with an entirely new question: what motivated these monkeys to persevere?

At the time of this experiment (again, a long time ago), scientists were well aware of two main factors that motivate people to take action. The first is physical or biological influences (like hunger, thirst, or safety). The second is gaining a reward or avoiding a punishment (like earning a good grade, getting an A on a test, or avoiding lunch detention). But neither of these influences explained why the monkeys continued their effort to solve the puzzles. They did not earn food, a pat on the back, or a reward, and they didn't get punished for not doing the puzzles. They just completed the puzzles over and over again on their own, and finished them faster and faster, and more efficiently each time. This discovery led to what psychologists refer to as **INTRINSIC MOTIVATION,** which we now know is a third factor that explains why people work toward a goal. It means that you are motivated to do something because it is internally satisfying for you, not because someone else or something else is trying to get you to do it. Pursuing something because you are intrinsically motivated also leads to greater persistence and willingness to stay engaged.

 IN OTHER WORDS, INTRINSIC MOTIVATION CREATES GRIT AND A GROWTH MINDSET.

So how can you tap into your intrinsic motivation? We want you to do well for the sake of doing well— but of course, it's easier to be motivated for some things than others. And school isn't always at the top of the list! Let's look at what motivation is so we can figure out how to grow it.

What is motivation and what causes it?

Motivation is what drives us to do something. That means it's key to all the things we've already talked about: developing a plan to meet goals, practicing grit, and having a growth mindset. You can be motivated by more than one thing at a time. For example, you might be motivated to go to bed earlier because you are really tired after a long day of school and after-school activities (a basic, physical factor), and also because you want to get up early to study for an exam the next day (a more complex desire for achievement).

Motivation can come from within you, or it can come from someone else. Not everyone has the same type or level of motivation in each situation. **PEOPLE ARE MOTIVATED BY LOTS OF THINGS**. We're going to talk about six categories:

- People, a sense of belonging
- Praise, attention, & approval
- Independence (control over your own decisions)
- Reward
- Achievement
- Interest

We are usually driven by more than one type of motivation. For example, we were motivated to write this book to share what we think is important to know in middle school *and* because we were excited to work on a project and create the book together!

Quiz

What motivates us changes throughout our life—and even from day to day or situation to situation. But people usually have a few things that are more likely to motivate them. Do you have an idea which of the six categories motivates you the most?

MOTIVATOR SELF-QUIZ

Grab a piece of paper and a pencil. Read the descriptions of each category and think about how much each motivates you. Give yourself a rating on a scale of 1-5 for each category, with 1 being only very slightly motivated by that, and 5 being highly motivated.

PEOPLE/SENSE OF BELONGING

If you are highly motivated by being with people, you likely spend a lot of time with friends. You enjoy group work, belonging to clubs, and organized team sports, and part of your identity reflects the groups to which you belong.

PRAISE/ATTENTION/APPROVAL

If you are highly motivated by attention and praise, other people's impression of you matters a lot. You also like to please your parents, friends, and teachers. You enjoy being recognized for your effort and accomplishments, including your grades.

INDEPENDENCE

Some people are motivated by the ability to set their own course and make decisions for themselves. Although you recognize the importance of working with others, you are most comfortable establishing your own structure, tackling projects, and making decisions on your own. You enjoy taking on responsibilities and being a leader in group settings.

REWARD

Some people are most motivated if they have something they are looking forward to after completing the task. If treating yourself to something you enjoy can help you push through when you feel like giving up (like the First–Then strategy in Chapter 2), you are probably motivated by rewards.

ACHIEVEMENT

Some people are motivated by their own personal sense of accomplishment. If you are highly motivated by excellence, you're driven by the desire to accomplish your goals, master skills, and improve yourself. You likely set high standards for yourself, and often challenge yourself to improve on previous performances.

INTEREST

This category is a little different from the others, because interest is a motivator for everyone! People naturally want to know more about topics that they find interesting, and are less motivated by things they do not find interesting. However, being motivated by interest means that you are generally curious and inquisitive, find many subjects interesting, and generally like to ponder (and answer) "why" questions.

MOTIVATION IS THE FIRST STEP IN WORKING
TOWARD YOUR GOALS.

Let's take a look at the crew's experience with motivation and how they responded:

MOTIVATION	ACTION PLAN
Dillon is motivated to not let his teammates down (people), because he feels a responsibility towards his team to keep improving his skills (achievement)...	so, he goes to the batting cages every weekend to practice.
Carlo is motivated by his love of art (interest) and his desire for people to praise his work (attention) and to win the art competition (reward)...	so, he spends several hours watching videos about how to use digital art software.
Bryce is motivated by getting good grades (achievement) and her passion for science (interest)...	so, she asks her teacher if she can do a more detailed experiment that she saw online.
Maddie is motivated by interactions with others (people). She wants to go to a movie on Saturday evening with her friends (reward)...	so, she completes her history project during the day on Saturday.
AJ wants their parents to stop asking how they are doing in math class (independence)...	so, they ask their parents to stop asking about their grades so long as AJ agress to share an update every other week.

What's a goal you're motivated to accomplish? What action steps do you need to take to reach that goal?

WHEN IT NO LONGER FEELS LIKE MOTIVATION... IT'S PROBABLY PRESSURE.

Sometimes things that seem like motivators start to become overwhelming and even feel uncomfortable. When that happens, it is no longer considered motivation: it's actually *pressure*. **PRESSURE IS THE UNPLEASANT EXPERIENCE OF FEELING LIKE YOU HAVE TO MEET AN EXPECTATION IN A WAY THAT CREATES STRESS.** It can cause a loss of excitement, enthusiasm, and momentum, and can even make you avoid doing the work. You might feel pressure when you are pushed to do something (for example, entering a math competition when you don't feel fully prepared). Pressure can also feel like intimidation or even a threat (for example, you can't go out with your friends if you don't get an A on your math test). When you are under pressure, do you wonder where it's coming from? Let's talk about two forms of pressure: pressure from others and self-driven pressure.

PRESSURE FROM OTHERS	SELF–DRIVEN PRESSURE
Your parent or caregiver might say: • Nothing less than an A is acceptable. • You should be in all honors classes. • You're so smart you should be in calculus by your senior year.	You might set unrealistic goals: • I need to get above 95% in every class this marking period, even though I have never gotten straight As. • I need to join three after school clubs this year.
Your coaches and others running extracurricular activities might say: • I expect you to practice several hours a day. • This sport (or activity) should take priority over other areas of your life. • You cannot miss a meeting/practice no matter what else is going on in your life.	You might engage in negative self-talk and self-criticism: • I'm a failure. • I'm terrible at school. • I will never get a good grade in this class. • I'm so stupid. • I'm not smart enough and probably won't even get into a college.
Your teachers might say: • You have to complete 40 math problems tonight. • The test is going to be very hard. • You need to try harder. • You should expect to spend a lot of time on this. • You should know the answer to that question.	You might be perfectionistic or inflexible in your thinking: • I have to be perfect. • It has to be exactly right. • If I mess this up, I will never forgive myself. • I got a 98% on my test but that was not good enough.

Your peers might say:

- Come on, let's skip class.
- You have to come, everyone is going to go.
- I dare you to____.
- Come on, just buy it.
- You're really not going to come?
- Just text them!
- Who cares what the teacher will say?
- Just let me copy the answers. I won't tell.

You might compare yourself to your peers or others:

- I need to do as well as my friends.
- I need to do the same activities that my friends do.
- I need to take classes (even advanced classes) because my friends are taking them.
- I'm not doing well enough because others are ahead of me.
- My friend got a 100% on the test. I should have too.

Pressure from others makes you feel like you need to meet someone else's expectations. You're probably familiar with the term **peer pressure,** which is discussed a lot in school. It is the influence of others your age to do, think, or believe something. For example, a friend may try to convince you to skip class or use social media apps your parents have said you're not allowed to use. Peer pressure can also cause you to feel like you need to be taking harder classes or join in extra-curriculars so you are doing as much as others.

Pressure from others can also come from the adults in your life, such as your parents, caregivers, and teachers. Sometimes when your teachers or parents encourage you to do your best, they unintentionally cause pressure. Instead of being helpful, this pressure makes it harder for you to do well. For example, Bryce's parents said to her, "you're a great student and so smart. You could get all As because you're so talented." At first, Bryce smiled, but that quickly transitioned to worry and doubt as she thought, "but what if I can't get As?" While we know that parental involvement helps students do better in school, it can backfire if it's too intense or ends up feeling like pressure. You should allow your parents to be a part of your educational journey so they can help you deal with some of the challenges, but we also encourage you to talk openly with them if they are making you feel pressured. (Check out the Tool Box at the end of this chapter to learn how to express the pressure you're feeling.)

Self-driven pressure comes from (you guessed it) within you, and comes from the belief that there is a goal you must achieve in a specific way. This form of pressure can sometimes be difficult to distinguish from motivation, but it typically includes **NEGATIVE SELF-TALK (SELF-CRITICISM), SOCIAL COMPARISONS, PERFECTIONISM,** and **THINKING ERRORS**. Let's go through each:

- **NEGATIVE SELF-TALK (SELF-CRITICISM),** which we discussed in Chapter 1, is the negative and insulting comments you make to yourself about your abilities. This is when you put yourself down, label yourself, and blame yourself for not doing better.

- **SOCIAL COMPARISONS** are when you evaluate your abilities, personality, or even the way you look in comparison to other people, and since you generally compare yourself to those who are doing better than you, you feel badly for coming up short. A better goal is to compare yourself with yourself, to see the progress you are making over time.

- **PERFECTIONISM** is when you have high, unrealistic standards for yourself that are often extremely difficult or impossible to attain. Perfectionists have a hard time celebrating their achievements and feeling good about themselves.

- **THINKING ERRORS** are irrational beliefs that lead to self-defeating thoughts and feelings. They often involve negative self-talk, self-criticism, and unhealthy comparisons to others, and can cause anxiety and depression. Take a look at five common thinking errors in the box.

☐ **CATASTROPHIZING:** When you think things are much worse than they actually are. It's when you have some negative thoughts or encounter a minor obstacle that quickly becomes a disaster in your mind. It often comes up as "What if..." thinking.
Example: Your coach didn't start you for the baseball game this week. You then start to think, "What if I never make the team in high school?"

☐ **ALL–OR–NOTHING THINKING:** When you think about something based on the extremes. The situation is either good or bad, perfect or a failure, with nothing in between. All-or-nothing thinking makes it hard to be flexible.
Example: You got a B on your first math test for the marking period and now feel like you are failing math.

☐ **FILTERING:** When you focus on the negatives and ignore the positives of a situation.

Example: You got your test back and you scored a 93%, but all you can think about are the points taken off for spelling.

☐ **SHOULDS:** When you have several rules for yourself and/or others. It often comes up as "I should..." or "shouldn't."
   Example: When you believe you *should* always know the answer to a teacher's question and *shouldn't* make any careless mistakes.

☐ **OVERGENERALIZING:** When you make a negative conclusion about something based on one piece of information or one part of an event.
   Example: Your teacher asked you to stop talking during the lesson, so now you think that teacher doesn't like you.

Take a Minute!

Do any of these thinking errors sound like you? Keep in mind that everyone makes thinking errors; the goal is to understand the ones you make the most, so you can get good at challenging them. We'll talk about these again, so make a note of which thinking errors you tend to make!

REALITY CHECK! When you are getting too much pressure from yourself or someone else, it often causes stress, which can create negative physical and emotional reactions. The goal is to become good at recognizing when you are feeling stressed and be able to manage those thoughts and feelings by dealing with them proactively (something we'll go into more detail about in Chapter 8).

THE EFFECTS OF PRESSURE

Pressure can lead to negative social and emotional consequences. High demands from teachers, parents, or coaches can cause you to feel like you're not good enough. It can also put strain on these relationships, and you might hesitate to seek advice from that person in fear of disappointing them, receiving a negative reaction, or even getting into trouble. Then, the pressure to perform becomes the focus, instead of just enjoying and benefitting from these healthy, meaningful relationships.

We mentioned that pressure from within can cause perfectionism and social comparisons. It's normal to compare yourself to others sometimes! We all do it. But when it becomes excessive, you

might start to see yourself as inferior (or superior),
or get stressed from the energy it takes to be in
constant competition with those around you. It
creates tension in your relationships with others.
For example:

- Bryce and her friends discuss their grades together.
  When a friend earns a higher grade, Bryce loses
  sight of her own accomplishments and thinks
  things like, "How did I not score as well as her? I'm
  never going to be the best in the class!"

- AJ frequently does very well on tests. When they
  notice that they do better than their peers, AJ will
  blurt out, "Wow, I'm glad I did better than you"
  which inadvertently makes others feel badly—and
  less close to AJ.

- Maddie's parents receive emails from her teachers
  about missing work and often say, "You want to
  do well in school, right? Why aren't you showing
  what we know you're capable of?"

Take a Minute!

1. Have you ever felt pressured by someone—a friend, parent, coach, or teacher?

2. Have you ever felt competitive when you compared yourself to your friends?

3. How did it make you feel? Did it change the relationship(s)?

PRESSURE TORNADO

LOW SELF-ESTEEM

NEGATIVE SELF-TALK

PERFECTIONISM

THINKING ERRORS

LACK OF CONFIDENCE

INCREASED STRESS AND ANXIETY

REDUCED PRODUCTIVITY OR PROCRASTINATION

There are many emotional consequences of feeling too much pressure....

WHEN THE PRESSURE BECOMES TOO POWERFUL, SELF-CRITICISM GROWS, AND SELF-CONFIDENCE AND SELF-ESTEEM DECLINE. It makes being a student so much harder. For lots of people, it also makes it really hard to be productive. When the pressure feels so intense that you are no longer productive, you might procrastinate or avoid doing the task altogether. (We'll discuss procrastination in more detail in Chapter 7.)

Students who have high expectations for their performance set competitive goals for school, sports, extracurricular activities, and more. Some kids find that pressure pushes them to try to achieve at whatever cost or to avoid the conflicts that come from pressure, particularly from others. They might:

- Work to the point of exhaustion
- Perform even when hurt or injured (like in sports)
- Copy another person's work (plagiarizing)
- Cheat

- Avoid work or turn things in late
- Lie to adults (who contribute to the pressure)

SELF-ADVOCACY TO REDUCE PRESSURE

Self-advocacy is the ability to communicate what you need and involves knowing your rights and being willing to defend them. Kids who practice self-advocacy are more likely to do well in school. It means you take responsibility for yourself and your learning. Here are some examples of when it is important to advocate for yourself:

- When you don't understand something you learned in class:
  - For example, you can ask your teacher, "It's not quite clear to me, can you please re-phrase that?"
- When you have questions about an upcoming test:
  - For example, talking to your teacher after class: "I really want to do well on the test, can you guide me on what to focus on when I study?" or "What's the best way to prepare for next week's test?"
- When you miss school, and you need to make up work:
  - For example, instead of waiting for the teacher

to remind you what work you have to complete, you touch base with each teacher to make a plan.

- When you are feeling overwhelmed or need help solving a problem:

    - For example, when your teacher assigns a project and you don't know where to start. You could say, "I have so many ideas floating around in my head, and I don't know what to do first. Can you [parents, friend, or teacher] please help me get started?"

- When you feel pressured or misunderstood by a friend, teacher, parent, or other adult:

    - For example, when a friend wants you to hang out but you know you need to study, you could say "I wish I could hang out tonight, but it would be a better choice for me to get some studying done today."

- When you recognize that you are putting pressure on yourself:

    - At some point in their life or school career, everyone compares themselves to others around them. When you compare yourself to your peers and think you aren't good enough, practice self-compassion by reminding yourself, "Take a deep breath. It's going to be okay, let's take it one step at a time. It's important to tap into my growth mindset when I'm feeling this way."

MASTERING MOTIVATION TOOL BOX

Now that you have a better understanding of the differences between motivation and pressure, let's go through some strategies.

TOOL 1: PRIORITIZE MOTIVATION

Motivation helps you achieve your goals, while pressure slows you down and makes it difficult to continue. So naturally, we want to help you focus on prioritizing motivation.

Remember the six categories of motivation?

1. People, a sense of belonging

2. Praise, attention, & approval

3. Independence (control over your own decisions)

4. Reward

5. Achievement

6. Interest

Look back at the activity where you rated which motivators were strongest and used the most often for you. Then, try to find some school-related goals you can apply them to. When you know which forms of motivation work best for you, you can apply them to an assignment or school-related goal. For example, if you are someone who is motivated by reward, you could set up a check-box list to highlight and celebrate what you accomplished. Seeing your progress tracked on paper as you move through it builds more motivation. Check out more examples in the motivation table.

PRAISE, ATTENTION AND APPROVAL

If you find praise motivating, be sure to acknowledge your accomplishments.

- Share your accomplishments with your family.

- Engage in positive self-talk.

PEOPLE, SENSE OF BELONGING

If this is your motivator, find ways to work with people instead of alone.

- Choose a friend to be your study buddy. You can study together or help keep each other on track and motivated.

- Choose group work when given the choice.

REWARD

If rewards motivate you most, try the First-Then strategy from Chapter 2.

- Give yourself five minutes of technology or a 10 minute walk in nature after crossing something off your to-do list.

- Get your chores/ homework done and then go chill with your friends or watch a video.

INDEPENDENCE

If this is your motivator, find ways to make decisions and speak your mind.

- When working with a group, try to take on a leadership role where you can make decisions.

- Trust your instincts. It's okay to choose to work alone instead of with a partner or friend if that's your preference.

ACHIEVEMENT

If this is your motivator, engage in activities that emphasize your accomplishments.

- Participate in activities that have a clear end goal (science fair, art show, essay contest, etc.).

- Monitor your personal achievements and create new goals.

INTERESTS

Everyone is more motivated when the task is interesting. Start paying attention to things that spark your interest.

- When assigned a research project, choose a topic you want to learn about.

- Thoughtfully choose activities that seem exciting to you.

When you find it hard to motivate yourself, it's time to practice self-advocacy. Check out how in Tool #2!

TOOL #2 SELF-ADVOCACY

When you feel pressured by others (whether it's by parents, other adults, or peers), practice self-advocacy and let them know. The keys to effective self-advocacy are:

1. Recognize when you feel the pressure.

2. Use "I-statements" to explain how the pressure is affecting you. I-statements allow you to express your needs using the words "I feel" or "I think."

3. Identify what needs to change to turn the pressure into positive motivation instead.

Take a look at how Maddie, Bryce, and Carlo did it.

MADDIE said to her parents: "Mom and Dad, I appreciate your support to do well in school, but sometimes I feel stressed when you tell me to 'try harder.' I think it would be more helpful if you focus on what I am doing well."

BRYCE told her friends: "I feel like I've been putting a lot of pressure on myself lately, and I am starting to feel really stressed. It might be better for me not to compare my grades to yours, so if I ask you how you did on the test, can you please remind me not to ask?"

CARLO told his parents: "I am ready and motivated to show you I can be responsible. I feel stressed when you remind me of my chores and schoolwork every day, and would like the chance to get my things done without being reminded."

This is just one example of how to self-advocate. We'll talk about it more in Chapter 9.

TOOL #3 CATCH AND REVERSE THE THINKING ERRORS

Remember **POSITIVE SELF-TALK** from Chapter 1 about mindsets? Guess what: we have another opportunity for you to use it! **POSITIVE SELF-TALK AND POSITIVE THINKING HELPS WHEN DEALING WITH PRESSURE.** Once you get good at challenging your thinking errors, it will become easier to have new automatic thoughts, which can be positive or just neutral. The first step is to notice when you are making a thinking error.

Step 1. Identify the thinking errors that you tend to make (we all have our favorites!) and when you are likely to make them.

Step 2. Practice catching yourself in the act: call yourself out when you're making a thinking error ("Oh there I go again... catastrophizing!").

Step 3. Remind yourself that a thinking error is just that: an error. It's not accurate or correct (it's faulty thinking!).

Step 4. Challenge and **replace** the thinking error by coming up with new thoughts. Add positive self-talk and self-compassion (go back to the list of positive self-talk in Chapter 1 for some ideas).

TOOL #4: TAP INTO YOUR "INNER MONKEY"

When there is too much pressure to perform, the
goal becomes about doing well for others, rather
than solving a problem for the joy of simply figuring
it out. Do you remember the monkeys from the
beginning of the chapter who had intrinsic drive to
solve the puzzle? Now it's time to tap into your "inner
monkey" and try learning something because you
want to know more about it. Discover the joy and fun
of creating for the sake of creating (not being graded
or judged, not even showing your final product to
anyone). Here are some ideas:

- Do an art project with materials you have not used
  before.
- Watch a TedTalk about something you are not
  familiar with.
- Do a jigsaw puzzle.
- Try a sport you've never played before.
- Learn a new card game.
- Try cooking a new food.
- Explore nature to learn about animals or plants.
- Look up more information about a topic you
  found interesting in school.

In this chapter, you learned about motivation, the negative effects of pressure, and how to be an advocate for yourself. You also got some specific tools to reduce pressure and increase motivation.

 **NOW IT'S TIME TO ACTIVATE YOUR MOTIVATION TO LEARN HOW TO NAVIGATE YOUR WAY AROUND MIDDLE SCHOOL IN CHAPTER 4!**

Chapter 4

Teachers and Schedules and Materials, Oh My!

$\mathcal{T}$ ake a moment to consider the changes in your environment that are probably new for you this year. Whether this is your first year in a new building or your first year in middle school—or even if you are in the same school but have new teachers—you will probably encounter some more complicated demands this year. In this chapter, we will talk about what you can expect as you **NAVIGATE THE MIDDLE SCHOOL BUILDING ITSELF,** as well as maneuver your way through dealing with multiple teachers each day.

You might feel like you are in over your head at first—middle school can certainly seem like a strange new land! Let's take a look at some of the crew's fears before starting school this year, what they realized, and how they dealt with their concerns.

DILLON'S BIGGEST CONCERN THIS YEAR WAS ABOUT THE SCHEDULE.

CLASS	TIME	Mon	Tue	Wed	Thu	Fri
1	8:00-9:26	A	B	A	B	A/B
2	9:33-11:00	B	A	B	A	A/B
3	11:30-11:55	A	B	A	B	A/B
4	12:00-1:26	B	A	B	A	A/B

He wondered things like:

- I heard we will have a block schedule...What does that mean?
- What electives should I choose?
- What classes do I need to take?
- Will any of my friends be in my classes?
- Where will I sit?
- What is "homeroom?"

The structure of your day might look a little different this year, and if you're like Dillon, you might wonder what those differences are. First, here are some common terms for school schedules:

- A **"ROTATING SCHEDULE"** means that the time of day that your classes (or "periods") meet changes, or rotates to different times of the day depending on the day of the week. For example, your last class one day might be your first class the next day.

- A **"BLOCK SCHEDULE"** means that instead of having 7 or 8 classes each day, you only have 3 or 4 classes, but they are longer, and you have different ones different days.

- Some middle schools have **"HOMEROOM"** or **"ADVISORY,"** a special class that doesn't focus on academics. It is often the first or last class of the day and focuses on organization, announcements, or special events.

- **"CORE CLASSES"** are the main academic classes, including English/language arts, science, social studies/history, and math. They are the classes that all students are required to take.

- **"ELECTIVES"** are classes that you get to choose that are not a part of the core curriculum. Electives usually include languages, arts, technology, or music/band classes.

You won't have a choice in how the middle school schedule works or in the core classes you will take, but you will get some say in your electives and maybe even where you sit in your classes. In some middle schools, you will have the same teacher (or two) for all of your core classes and change classes for your electives. In most middle schools, however, all of your classes will be taught by a different teacher in different classrooms. This means you could be changing classes up to 8 times each day!

Here is some advice on how to manage the schedule that helped Dillon:

- Choose electives based on what interests you, not what your friends want you to take. You can learn information about the elective on your school website. Don't let other people pressure you into taking something you aren't excited about because, first, you are in it all year, and second, you may not even have the class with them.

- If your teachers let you choose where you sit, choose wisely. Sitting next to your friends or the window can be fun, but it can also be distracting. Consider a seat close to the teacher, in the middle of the room, and away from distractions.

BRYCE WAS MOST CONCERNED ABOUT FINDING HER WAY AROUND THE SCHOOL BUILDING AND GETTING TO CLASS ON TIME.

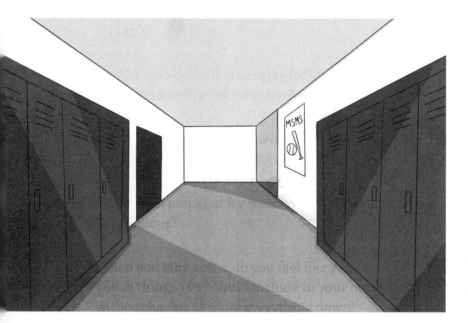

She wondered things like:

- How will I find my classes?
- How will I have time to get to my locker between classes?
- The building is so much bigger, will I get lost?
- What if I'm late for class?
- Will I get in trouble for being late?

Have you had worries like these? **TAKE A DEEP BREATH, AND DON'T PANIC!** Regardless of what you're worried about, whether it's getting to classes on time, figuring out your locker, the amount of work... soon enough, everything will feel natural and not so hard after all. With some planning, you will have enough time between classes to get from one side of the building to the other if you don't dawdle. The hallways are crowded, though, and people will be going in both directions so that they can take the shortest route to their next class. Just like traffic on the road, try to stay to the right side of the hallway and be aware of people trying to pass you. Often, middle schools have certain classrooms grouped together, in hallways dedicated to specific grade levels (maybe there's a 6th-grade hall) or specific subjects (like a math hall). Rooms should also have room numbers that go in order, usually with numbers in the 100s on the first floor, 200s on the 2nd floor, etc.

Here are some suggestions that helped Bryce feel more comfortable:

- Look for **VISUAL LANDMARKS** to help you remember where certain classrooms are so that you can find them more easily when the hallways are crowded (for example, Bryce took note that her science classroom is the 2nd door on the left after the bathroom in Hallway A).

- If you tend to get lost, **PAIR UP WITH A PEER** who has the next class with your or near yours.

AJ WAS SUPER CONCERNED ABOUT USING LOCKERS (AND LOCKS) FOR THE FIRST TIME.

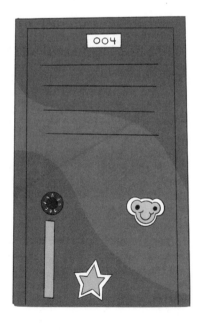

They worried about things like:

- I'll have so many books they won't fit in my backpack.
- Do I have to carry my instrument around all day?
- What if I bring the wrong things to class?
- What if I can't get my locker open?

Using lockers in middle school is like a rite of passage—an exciting one! Lockers are a place to store the things you can't (or don't want to) lug around with you all day, like books, notebooks, instruments, sports equipment, jackets, and extra supplies. In most schools, you can even decorate inside your locker to show off your style! Lockers don't have a ton of space, but some things you might want to keep in your locker are:

- "emergency supply kit" (extra pencils, pens, batteries for calculator, etc.)
- notebooks, textbooks, and electronic devices that you don't need to bring with you to the class you are currently in
- a mirror, photos of family, friends, pets, etc., and other personal touches

- white board (for reminders and notes to yourself about things you need to bring home with you)
- lunch, if you bring it

Once you get your schedule, you can plan out your route around the building to each of your classes to see when you pass your locker. We suggest that you start each day at your locker, and take the materials you need for a few classes. Then swap them with the materials you need for the next few classes when you pass by your locker or have a lunch break. Go to your locker at the end of each day before you leave school to make sure you bring home everything you need for your homework. Keeping your locker organized and using a system to easily and quickly pick up the materials you need when you stop by are helpful (see the Toolbox at the end of this chapter).

Most kids can open their lockers easily most of the time once they've memorized the combination and practiced opening the lock. Sometimes AJ has a nightmare about not being able to get their locker open or forgetting the combination. Fortunately, once AJ wakes up, they use positive self-talk to remind themselves that it's unlikely, but if it does happen, it's not a catastrophe because their homeroom teacher has their combination written down, just in case they need it. It's a good idea for a teacher to know your combination if you need a reminder, but you shouldn't share your combination with anyone else, even your friends.

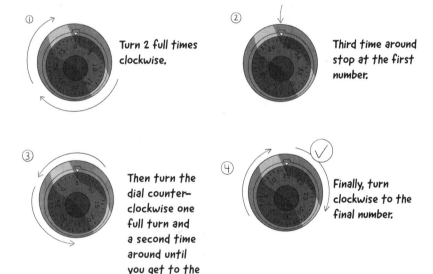

① Turn 2 full times clockwise.

② Third time around stop at the first number.

③ Then turn the dial counter-clockwise one full turn and a second time around until you get to the second number in the combination.

④ Finally, turn clockwise to the final number.

CARLO WAS FEELING VERY ANXIOUS ABOUT HOW MUCH HOMEWORK HE WAS GOING TO HAVE AND HOW HE WOULD MANAGE TO GET ALL OF HIS WORK DONE.

He had thoughts like:

- Will I have a lot more work this year?
- I don't really like to read. What if I can't keep up with the reading assignments?
- Will my classes be hard?
- Will I have a lot of homework?

There's going to be more work in middle school than there was in elementary school! That's just a fact. With more teachers, you might have more homework each night and be expected to keep track of your assignments more independently this year. Using a planner, agenda, or calendar can help you keep track of your assignments. It's pretty common for new middle school students to be doing well at first, and then, all of a sudden, their grades drop. With more demands on your time, responsibilities, and expectations in middle school, a temporary dip in grades is not unusual—it's what you do to bring yourself out of that dip that counts. Be your own detective to figure out what is going well and what isn't so you can get yourself out of that cycle. Remember that your grades are not the only thing that matters: the learning process is also essential.

REALITY CHECK! The fact is that with several teachers giving you assignments instead of just one, they may not be aware of what days you have a lot due or have tests in other classes. This means there might be days where you don't have a lot of homework, and some days where you have homework in most (or all) of your classes, or even multiple tests on the same day. When that happens, you will probably feel pressure, which is a perfect time to practice those self-advocacy skills we talked about in Chapter 3. ☺

Carlo has some tips for success that help him when he is struggling to keep up with the workload:

- **WRITE DOWN ALL OF YOUR ASSIGNMENTS,** even if you think you will remember what to do. Carlo writes them on a large desk calendar, so he can easily see what's coming up.

- **PUT YOUR NAME AND THE DATE ON ALL OF YOUR PAPERS.** Neatness counts. Take time to proofread.

- **DO YOUR HOMEWORK** (not just for the sake of doing it, but as a form of deliberate practice of the information), and turn it in on time.

- **KEEP YOUR PAPERS ORGANIZED** so that you can find what you need easily.

MADDIE'S BIGGEST CONCERN THIS YEAR WAS ABOUT HOW SHE WOULD MANAGE HAVING A DIFFERENT TEACHER FOR EACH SUBJECT.

She kept thinking things like:

- *I've never had so many teachers at one time before...*
- *How will I deal with so many teachers?*
- *How will I know what my teachers expect of me?*
- *What if the teachers are mean?*

Kids who get along with their teachers tend to be more comfortable asking questions and getting extra help when they need it. That makes it easier to understand new material and do your best on tests and projects. You can help build a good relationship with your teachers by being respectful of the teacher and your classmates. You can show respect by raising your hand when you want to contribute, listening to what's being said, following rules, asking when you have questions, showing you are actively engaged with your body language, and using the resources you have (like looking at the syllabus for information about class expectations and content instead of waiting for the teacher to tell you what's coming up). None of that sounds new, right? But since middle school teachers see you for less time each day and have a lot more students than elementary teachers, it takes longer for them to get to know you—which means that you need to advocate for yourself by asking questions when you don't understand something.

Take a Minute!

What do you think your teachers expect from their students? What are some things that are good for teachers *and* students?

TEACHERS WANT TO HELP THEIR STUDENTS, but the reality is that there is not always enough time during class to answer everyone's questions. If you don't have time to ask all of your questions during class, then consider going to your teacher outside of class time to get extra help (at lunchtime, before or after school, during your free period, etc.). Try to be specific about what help you are asking for (for example, "I am not sure what to write about in the essay you assigned, can I schedule a time to talk with you for a few minutes about the ideas I have so that you can help me choose one?"). Being responsible for your learning also means having a back-up plan for when you have questions about assignments and your teacher is not available. (We'll talk about this in a minute with Tool #2!)

USE THE TOOLS YOU LEARNED IN CHAPTER 3 TO HELP YOU SELF-ADVOCATE WHEN YOU HAVE A QUESTION!

 PREPARING FOR SCHOOL TOOLBOX

TOOL #1: COLOR COORDINATE

Try color-coordinating your school supplies so that everything that you need for one class is easily visible. For example, if you choose green for science, use something green to indicate "science" on each of your materials that relate to that class. When you need to get all of your science materials, you can quickly scan for all of the green-colored items in your locker or bag. Some ideas for color coordinating:

- choosing a different colored notebook for each class

- using folders of different colors for each of your classes

- writing the class name in that color ink on the front of a folder or spiral notebook, if the folder or notebook itself isn't that color

- labeling the corresponding sections of your binder with the color you chose for each class

- covering your textbooks with paper (or labels) using the color you chose for each class
- using stickers, labels, or washi tape in the corresponding colors

TOOL #2: MAKE A BACK-UP PLAN

The purpose of a back-up plan is so you know what to do if you hit a "bump in the road" and things don't work out the way you planned. Back-up plans are a way for you to use your growth mindset to problem-solve, self-advocate and show independence and responsibility for your work.

What is your back-up plan for each of your classes? If you are confused or don't have materials that you need, what can you do? Can you email the teacher? Is there a website you can check? Is there a friend in your class you can call? Take a moment now to think about someone in each of your classes that can be part of your back-up plan, and make list on a separate sheet of paper with their contact information.

TOOL #3: SCOPE OUT THE SCHOOL BEFORE YOUR FIRST DAY

Before school starts, many schools will organize a new student orientation day, which is a great opportunity to be able to visit the school to do a walk-through and look around the building. Even if your school doesn't do this, contact the office before school starts and they should be able to give you a map and your schedule (or at least be able to tell you where your classes are likely to be), even if they can't give you the exact order. Make a note of the places you will need the location of (like the nurse's office, the front office, stairwells, the gym, the cafeteria, the bathrooms, etc.).

Hopefully you feel a little bit better about your journey navigating through the middle school building and multiple teachers, and you have some tools that you can use to help you feel even more confident. **NEXT, WE'LL BE EXPLORING HOW YOU LIKE TO LEARN, IN CHAPTER 5: LOTS OF LEARNING STYLES.**

Chapter 5

Lots of Learning Styles

*D*id you know there are actually a bunch of different ways that people learn? Just like how people have different tastes in music or clothing, most of us also have preferences about how we like to learn new things and make sense of the world around us. In this chapter, we'll investigate how you like to learn and experiment with ways to use your styles in the best way.

TAKING IN INFORMATION

No matter who we are or how old we are, we learn about the world around us by taking in information through our senses. Both inside and outside of school, the three most common ways that people take in new information are:

- auditory pathway (through our ears),
- visual pathway (through our eyes), and
- kinesthetic pathway (through touch and movement).

VISUAL EXAMPLES	AUDITORY EXAMPLES	KINESTHETIC EXAMPLES
Charts	Class discussions	Experiments
Diagrams	Teacher instruction	Hands-on activities
Illustrations	Audio books	Taking notes
Reading		

Usually, we're using multiple pathways (senses) at the same time. Many people feel equally comfortable learning new things all three ways, but some people have a strong preference for one over another. Having a strong favorite for one of the pathways means that learning that way is more natural and enjoyable for you, which is usually more motivating (remember the importance of motivation from Chapter 3?).

Quiz

Do you naturally lean toward one pathway for learning new information over another? Take this quiz to find out! Remember, there are no right or wrong answers to this quiz, so just answer the questions as honestly as you can. Number a paper from 1 to 24. Then, read the question prompts and write down which answer is the most like what you would do.

NOTE: We know that there will be questions where you will want to pick more than one answer, but try to choose the one option that is the most true for you the most often. If you have difficulty choosing between two answers because they are both equally true for you, it's OK to pick them both (but put a ✓ next to that question number on your paper).

1. Which of these classroom activities do you like best?

> **a.** class discussions

> **b.** reading or looking at illustrations in the textbook

> **c.** demonstrations or experiments

2. If you were going to pick up a book to read for fun in your free time, would you rather read...

> **a.** a non-fiction or fiction novel

> **b.** a graphic novel

> **c.** a book with word searches, crossword puzzles, or other non-story book

3. Which of these things would you be more likely to do to help you figure out how to spell a word?

a. spell it out loud to see if it sounds right

b. write it down a few different ways to see which looks right

c. "air write" with your finger to see if it feels right

4. If you have to wait in line to make a purchase, what are you most likely to spend your time doing while you wait your turn?

a. talking to or eavesdropping on the people near you

b. looking at the items near you

c. fidgeting with something you are holding or moving around in place

5. When you see the word "dog," which of these things are you most likely to do first?

a. say the word "dog" to yourself

b. form a mental image of a dog in your mind's eye

c. think about being with a dog (how it feels, what it does, how it makes you feel, etc.)

6. When learning how to use a new electronic device, you would be most likely to...

    a. get someone to tell you how to use it

    b. get someone to show you how to use it

    c. figure it out for yourself

7. If you went to a dance or event at your school, what would you remember most about it afterwards?

    a. what you talked about

    b. the people you saw there

    c. the dance moves you did

8. What do you find most distracting when you are trying to study?

    a. people talking or other noise near where you are working

    b. people walking past where you are working

    c. sitting in an uncomfortable place

9. When in a new place, how would you prefer to find your way around?

a. ask someone for directions

b. look at a map or diagram

c. wander until you find where you want to be

10. Which of these three elective classes is your favorite?

a. Music

b. Art

c. PE

11. Which of these do you most like to do to relax?

a. listen to music

b. watch TV

c. exercise (walk, run, shoot hoops, etc.)

12. If you had to try to memorize a friend's phone number, which of these would work best for you?

    a. saying it out loud several times

    b. trying to picture it in your head

    c. writing it down several times

13. When you hear a song that you like, which of these are you most likely to do?

    a. sing along

    b. imagine the video that goes with the song

    c. dance or tap your foot to the beat

14. Which of these would you prefer as a present?

    a. a music download

    b. a poster or a book

    c. a game or piece of sports equipment

15. Which of these activities would you rather do with your friends?

   a. go to a concert

   b. go to a movie

   c. play a sport

16. Which of these things do you find the most distracting when you are trying to concentrate?

   a. hearing noises around you

   b. lights being too bright or too dim

   c. being too hot or too cold

17. What are you likely to remember the most when you meet someone new?

   a. the sound of their voice

   b. how they looked

   c. what they did

18. If you were giving someone directions to your house, would you most likely...

    a. tell them the street names along the route

    b. tell them about the landmarks they will pass along the route

    c. draw them a map or diagram of the route

19. If you want to cook a special treat for a class party, you would be most likely to...

    a. ask a friend of family member for a recipe

    b. get ideas by looking at pictures in a cookbook or on social media

    c. make something that you have made before so that you don't need directions

20. You prefer websites/social media that have....

    a. audio clips

    b. video clips

    c. lots of things to click on

21. When you think about the answer to a test question, you are more likely to...

a. remember what your teacher said about the topic

b. remember what you read about the topic

c. remember what you wrote about the topic

22. When you think about your best friend, you first think about...

a. what they sound like

b. what they look like

c. how they act

23. When it comes to stories, you prefer...

a. to listen to them

b. to read them

c. to act them out

24. When you are thinking about a complicated math problem, it helps you most to...

a. talk it through with someone

b. draw a picture

c. move objects around

Now count up your answer choices and write the total number of each letter on your paper (if you chose more than one answer choice for any of the questions, count both answers).

If you had the highest number of As, you tend to be a more auditory learner. If you chose more Bs, you tend to be more of a visual learner, and if you chose more Cs, you gravitate toward a more kinesthetic way of learning. If your totals were pretty much even, you do not seem to have a strong preference for any of the learning modalities, which means that you can mix and match any of the tools at any time to give yourself some variety. If you did have a clear winner (or even two that stood out as preferences), try strategies that build on those preferences. In the toolbox at the end of this chapter, we have tools for each learning modality preference.

Take a Minute!

Did you make a ✓ next to any of the questions on the quiz because you had a hard time choosing between two answers? If so, take a minute to think about why it was hard for you to choose. Do you notice any patterns regarding situations when you would make one choice over another?

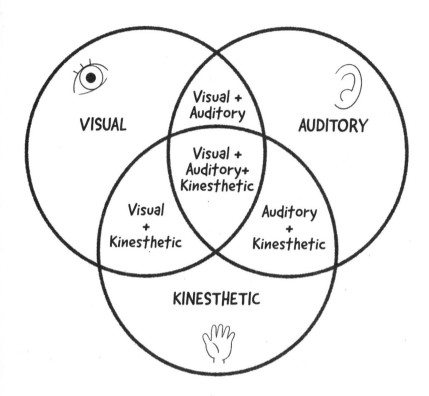

There's overlap between the learning pathways and the strategies and tools that work for each style. You're not limited to one type! Each of the members of the crew has their unique preferences—just like you do! Take a look at some of the preferences of Carlo, AJ, Maddie, Bryce, and Dillon.

Carlo prefers visual strategies. He easily can recall what things look like and create pictures in his mind, so he uses that to his advantage. He relies heavily on whether it "looks right" when he practices drawing landscapes and when he is spelling words. Diagrams, charts, and illustrations make sense to him and help him understand complex information. Timelines help him understand the sequence of historical events. He often draws pictures on paper when he is working through math problems and visualizes (makes pictures in his head) when he is reading.

Maddie has a preference for auditory learning. She isn't very good at remembering what people look like, but she easily remembers what they say, so she almost always remembers what the teacher says about homework assignments without having to look in her planner when she gets home. Maddie can easily memorize song lyrics and recognize tunes, so she uses that to help her memorize information for tests. Class discussions energize Maddie and help her pay attention.

Dillon has a strong preference for the kinesthetic style. Science concepts make the most sense to Dillon when he can engage in hands-on activities and he can move from his seat to the lab stations. Writing things out by hand helps him remember information better. He often brainstorms while shooting hoops because movement helps his brain consolidate and organize information.

AJ does not have a clear preference for any of the learning modalities. They use a combination of strategies that match all three styles. AJ relies on if notes "sound right" and finger placement "feels right" when learning to play an instrument. They remember songs easily, so they often use music as a tool to help them memorize information. AJ also likes to move around while practicing speeches or vocabulary because it helps them think. They enjoy reading physical books and listening to audiobooks. Looking at diagrams and charts helps them make quick sense of information.

Bryce prefers a combination of visual and kinesthetic inputs. She usually remembers what she sees, so she loves to look at pictures in her textbooks and uses manipulatives when solving math problems. Writing is an excellent way for her to combine her two preferences. Some of her favorite study tools are using flashcards, making sketches with captions, and recopying her notes using lots of colors.

 **Which of the tools and strategies that they use also work well for you?**

MAKING SENSE OF INFORMATION

There are also different ways we think about information once we have it. These **thinking styles** are the ways our brain naturally makes sense of and organizes information.

Take a Minute!

What is your thinking style? Take a look at the chart below and decide which of the types sound more like how you think about new information.

GLOBAL THINKERS TEND TO...	ANALYTICAL THINKERS TEND TO...
• be "big picture" thinkers • think about how things are connected • use stories to help clarify concepts • use real-world scenarios to help make sense of information • think about the main idea first, then pay attention to the small details • be excited about abstract concepts that do not always have a clear answer • be impatient with going one step at a time, in order	• be "detail-oriented" • like order and structure • be list-makers and complete tasks in sequential order • like to know the details first, then think about how they all work together to form the main idea • like order and sequences • like to think when it is quiet and prefer working alone over group work • like knowing what to expect

Of course, we don't process information in *only* one way. You probably use both global and analytical methods. In fact, thinking styles are on a continuum, and the way you process and organize information can change depending on the circumstances.

Your preferred learning pathway and the way you make sense of information both contribute to **YOUR OWN UNIQUE LEARNING STYLE.** Learning style is a personal preference, and it has nothing to do with ability. Ability is how well you can do something, while learning style is the *way* you choose to do it. The key is to be flexible and know how to make what you're learning fit your learning style, so you can set yourself up for success. The bottom line is, using a variety of strategies helps you learn and motivation has a huge impact on your learning.

We've asked you to think a lot about how you think! There is actually a name for that: **METACOGNITION.** Metacognition is being aware of, reflecting on, and evaluating your thinking, and then using that valuable information to make good choices about how you will tackle whatever challenges you face. Basically, it's thinking about thinking! Understanding your learning style is a part of metacognition, and it can help you in school because when you know what strategies work well for you, you can work more efficiently, use your time more effectively, and advocate for your needs.

REMEMBER, LEARNING STYLES ARE A PERSONAL PREFERENCE, AND STYLE PREFERENCES ARE NOT SYNONYMOUS WITH ABILITY. STYLE IS THE WAY YOU CHOOSE TO DO SOMETHING, NOT YOUR ABILITY TO DO IT WELL.

TEACHING STYLE

In the same way that you have your preferred learning style, teachers also have their own style preference. The subject matter and grade level that you are in affects the style teachers use to teach new information. In middle school (and beyond) information is usually presented visually or verbally. If you are a visual or auditory learner, that is great for you! But if those are not your preferred modes of learning, don't stress—you can still use simple strategies for school that build on your learning style. We will talk more about strategies specifically for note-taking and studying for tests in Chapter 6, but in the toolbox coming up, there are three simple strategies that can help bridge the gap between your learning style and your teacher's teaching style.

IF YOU DO HAVE A NATURAL PREFERRED LEARNING STYLE, BUILDING ON IT CAN HELP MAKE LEARNING FEEL EASIER, BECAUSE YOU'RE DOING IT IN A MORE COMFORTABLE WAY.

 ## LEARNING STRATEGY TOOLBOX

Now that you know a little more about the way you like to learn new information and the way that your brain naturally makes sense of the world around you, you can use some tools to set yourself up for success. Remember, the key is to use a *variety* of strategies and tools to help you learn, and to think about what works well and motivates you.

TOOL #1: SIXTY SECOND SKETCH

Try drawing during class! Let's be clear: we are not suggesting that you draw *instead of* paying attention to what the teacher is saying in class. But if you're a visual learner and pictures help you think, doodling *about* what the teacher is saying can help you make sense of the information being taught. One way is to make simple summary sketches to help your brain process information that you hear or read. Every so often, when you are reading or listening to a lecture, make a quick sketch that sums up the main idea or key information (take no more than 60 seconds to make your sketch).

TIPS:

Use stick figures → Use arrows ▭ box for important ideas

use simple shapes ☆ ▢ ♡ ○ ▷ ♡ • use bullets

* IT'S ABOUT IDEAS, NOT ART SKILLS.

Grab a pen!

Take a look at the examples on the next page of 60-second sketches Carlo made, then give it a try for yourself. Don't worry—you don't have to have any artistic talent to use this tool, it's just a way to be an active learner by incorporating your visual strengths.

CARLO'S WATER CYCLE

CHAPTER SUMMARY

RIP fake death

Poison

HISTORY TERM

Patriotism

TOOL #2: ACTIVELY PARTICIPATE IN DISCUSSIONS

If you are a more auditory learner, hearing information helps you make sense of it, so take advantage of that gift by discussing what you are learning, both in class and outside of class. Try retelling and summarizing aloud to a parent or friend outside of class. You can offer a summary statement during class as well, as a way of clarifying; for example, "So to think about how the Aztecs and Mayans were different,

we should focus on how each civilization ruled?"
Asking questions and taking part in discussions in
class not only shows the teacher that you are paying
attention, it also lets you take an active role in your
own learning—which can be very motivating!

TOOL #3: MOVE YOUR BODY

Let's face it, sitting in class all day is hard—especially
when your natural inclination is to move around! If
you are a more kinesthetic learner (or even if you just
need to help wake yourself up a bit when you find
the subject boring), moving can be really helpful to
keep your mind engaged. If you have the space and it
does not disrupt those around you, try moving your
body while you read or listen by pacing, tapping your

foot, or even bouncing a ball. You should definitely talk to your teacher and advocate for why this will be helpful first. For example, you could say, "I find it very helpful to move around when trying to learn. Would it be okay to stand up behind my chair and walk in place or get up and take a lap around the classroom?"

Of course, we're not saying that you should jump up and down and disturb the people around you. The options we mentioned for moving around are not realistic for all situations. You can use small, subtle movements that are respectful to your teacher and peers to help you stay alert during class time. For example, Dillon often silently squeezes a squish-ball or chews gum (when it isn't against the rules) while he listens or reads in class. At home, he rides a stationary bike while he brainstorms ideas for projects and essays because that helps his thoughts flow.

Take a Minute!

Reflect on how you could add these tools into your daily routines at school and at home. Which of those ideas grab your interest the most? Think about which strategies you already use and which ones you want to try adding into your daily habits.

REALITY CHECK! Let's be honest, the goal of school is to learn, and learning new information takes effort. Learning takes practice, perseverance, grit, and a growth mindset, but sometimes those things are not enough. Sometimes, even when we have grit and a growth mindset, a "roadblock" affects your ability to learn, pay attention, listen, read, write, express yourself, or do math. If that roadblock is a difference in how your brain processes information, you might have a *learning disability*. Having a learning disability means that it may take you longer to understand, store, or use information, but it does not mean that you can't learn and it has nothing to do with how smart you are. In fact, there are many people who have learning disabilities who are successful because of their grit and determination (see the extra resources section for places you can learn more about very successful famous people with learning disabilities). Learning disabilities affect people differently, and if you do have one, it is especially important for you to know yourself as a learner so that you can advocate for yourself by letting your teachers, family, and friends know how you learn best.

IF YOU DO SUSPECT THAT SOMETHING IS GETTING IN THE WAY OF YOUR LEARNING, WE ENCOURAGE YOU TO TALK TO YOUR TEACHER OR PARENT/GUARDIAN. Specialized testing by trained professionals can help pinpoint what is causing your difficulty and help you learn strategies and identify accommodations to manage it.

HAVING A LEARNING DISABILITY MEANS THAT IT MAY TAKE YOU LONGER TO UNDERSTAND, STORE, OR USE INFORMATION, BUT REMEMBER THAT IT DOESN'T MATTER WHAT ROAD YOU TAKE TO GET THERE, JUST THAT YOU GET THERE IN THE END.

Learning more about how you learn best and knowing that you can affect your own success gives you control over how you deal with new information. It also gives you some choice (and some responsibility) in your own education. By thinking about how you learn best, you can take the reins and make good choices that help you work more efficiently and effectively. And by doing that, you can make learning and school success easier...and more fun! In the next chapter, we'll explore more strategies for doing homework, taking notes, and studying for and taking tests.

Chapter 6

The Learning Strategies Superstore

Welcome to the Learning Strategies Superstore! Here, we'll create some work habits to make school less stressful. It'll be like having a "superstore" full of useful tools that will make it easier to learn. Lots of kids think they should just automatically know how to learn, study, and prepare for tests, but the truth is that most students need to learn how to do these things. So we're going to give you tips and strategies to work productively, take good notes, read with purpose, and show what you know on tests. If you aren't sure how to learn in the best way for you, this chapter (and the *super* tools in the toolbox) are here to help, so let's get started!

 **What do you think is the biggest worry most kids have about school?**

Most of the time, students (and parents!) are concerned about tests and grades. We'll let you in on something you might not know about tests and grades...they aren't important in the way you might think. The ultimate goal of school is for you to learn **how to learn**: how to memorize, organize, think about, and apply information to be an independent thinker, which will help you become a good, informed decision-maker as an adult. The test itself isn't what matters; tests are a way to measure how well the teachers are doing their jobs and how well you are doing your job as a learner. The grade you get on a test or a report card is not actually as important as what the grade represents—that you have a good understanding of the information. So it's what goes into *preparing* for the test (not the actual test) that matters.

AS ALBERT EINSTEIN SAID: "EDUCATION IS NOT THE LEARNING OF FACTS, BUT THE TRAINING OF THE MIND TO THINK."

HOW SHOULD YOU STUDY?

You've probably heard from adults around you that you need to "study," but do you really know what that means? You might already know that middle school requires more independence than elementary school. For example, in middle school:

- You will have more responsibility for **ORGANIZING YOUR MATERIALS**.

- You will be asked to **TAKE NOTES** on what you read in books and what the teachers teach during class.

- You will have to **MANAGE YOUR TIME** to do homework assignments for multiple teachers.

- You will be expected to **MEMORIZE MORE INFORMATION**, including specific dates, facts, and formulas.

- You will have to **STUDY FOR TESTS DIFFERENTLY**, because many test questions will focus less on simply *recalling* information (remembering facts) and more on *applying* the information you have learned.

The term "study skills" describes the work habits and strategies that people use when trying to learn or memorize something new. The classwork and homework assignments are the first step in learning new information. The next step is using effective study strategies on your own. Try out the quiz below to see how you approach studying.

STUDY SKILLS AND STRATEGIES

Quiz

Grab a piece of paper and a pencil and let's get started. Number your paper and read the questions for each section. Give yourself an honest rating; *hardly ever* is 1 point, *sometimes* is 2, and *almost always* is 3.

1. Do you prioritize your after-school activities so that schoolwork comes first?

2. Do you review your notes daily so you don't have to cram right before a test?

3. Do you know how to study what you've learned in a way that matches your particular learning style (for example, visual learners often learn from writing and drawing things out)?

4. Do you try to understand the material before memorizing the facts?

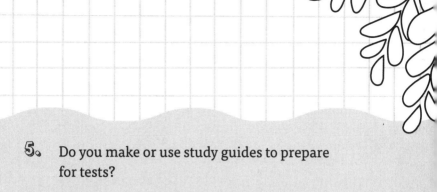

5. Do you make or use study guides to prepare for tests?

6. Do you have specific strategies for when you have to memorize information for a test?

7. Do you usually remember what you have studied when you are taking a test?

8. Do you feel prepared for tests, so that you don't feel anxious?

9. When you take notes, do you feel like you know which things you should include in your notes, without having to write everything down?

10. Do you go over your notes after taking them, to review or edit what you wrote?

Now add up your points. If your total is 24 or less, adding some new strategies to your routine will help you understand the information you are learning on a deeper level.

How do you know how much you need to study? There is (obviously!) a difference between knowing just a little about a topic and being an expert on a topic. Knowing just a little about a topic without a deep understanding is called a "surface understanding." In middle school (and beyond), you don't need to be an expert, but it's helpful to have more than just a surface understanding of what you're learning.

My teacher didn't remind me of these things.

He didn't tell me to take notes.

She only said that once.

No one told me to spend a lot of time on this.

How was I supposed to know it was going to be on the test?

How was I supposed to know it was important?

Have you ever had any thoughts like those after taking a test? If so, you're not alone—we hear similar complaints from students all the time! We aren't saying that there isn't some truth to those comments, but now that you are in middle school, knowing what (and when) to study is mostly your responsibility. Taking ownership of your learning shows you are responsible, and will also prepare you for high school.

Every year as you get older, I'm sure you hear the adults in your life telling you to be more responsible. Learning can be either passive or active. The truth is that the more effort you put in, the more likely you are to reach your goals, and the less effort you put in, the less likely success is.

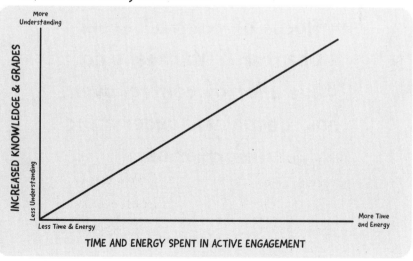

Time spent engaging in active learning leads to deeper understanding. If you don't yet have a deep understanding of a particular topic, how can you move from your current more surface-level understanding to where you actually "own" the information? The two best ways are to engage in deliberate, purposeful practice by using **ACTIVE LEARNING STRATEGIES**, and by being metacognitive.

Using **ACTIVE LEARNING STRATEGIES** means putting in the effort, energy, and time to reach your goals instead of sitting back and waiting to see what happens to you.

  Do you remember the term "locus of control" from Chapter 1? You really do have a lot of control over how deeply you understand information.

Take a look at the following chart for some examples of passive and active learning strategies. The examples on the left require less effort...but are also less effective.

PASSIVE LEARNING STRATEGY	VS.	ACTIVE LEARNING STRATEGY
You read the words in your textbook, just to get it done.	VS.	You annotate as you read (see Tool #1).
You read over your class notes because your teacher told you to.	VS.	You make flashcards from your notes and quiz yourself.
You sleep with math formulas under your pillow, hoping that will help you memorize them.	VS.	You write (and rewrite) the formulas while you say them out loud to yourself until you remember them.
You watch a video on the causes of the Revolutionary War, while texting your friend.	VS.	You watch the video, pausing to write down important information as you watch.
You do your practice set of math problems quickly, just to get your homework done.	VS.	You are metacognitive—you think about *why* you are doing each step in your math problems.

Using active learning strategies gets you closer to your goal of having a deeper understanding. In fact, research suggests that almost half of what we take in through our senses (including what we hear and read) is forgotten within an hour UNLESS we actively engage with it.

Take a Minute!

Take a look at the chart one more time. This time, as you read through the examples, think about which of the choices you do most often, and check in with yourself in an honest way about if you could take more responsibility for your learning.

REALITY CHECK! Learning is a process, and so is studying. Of course, not every learning or study strategy works equally well for everyone (remember learning style preferences!). Most people don't find the perfect study method on the first try—you need to be your own detective, trying out different strategies and refining the ones you like for different situations. We encourage you to try out some of the active learning strategies in the Toolbox at the end of this chapter.

TWO KEY STRATEGIES FOR LEARNING

There are two key strategies that will help make your middle school years successful: **ANNOTATING TEXT** and **TAKING NOTES.**

The Studies Show...

Studies have shown that while students who typed their notes tended to include more information and write more down, those who hand-wrote their notes had a better understanding of the information and were better able to remember what they wrote!

Of course, for some people, hand-writing takes so much longer that typing actually works better for them. Give the experiment a try yourself and see which way works best for you.

ANNOTATING

ANNOTATION means marking up a piece of text with words, symbols, and questions to help you be actively engaged with the information.

Some ways that you might want to annotate include:

- make **notes in the margins** to emphasize something you want to remember

- **circle words** you don't know (you can even look them up and write the definition in the margin near the word)

- **underline** something important

- **highlight** key names and/or dates

- write a **question mark** by anything confusing

- put an **exclamation mark** near something surprising

- make a note of **literary devices** that the author uses (foreshadowing, personification, metaphors, etc.)

- **draw a heart or smiley face** next to something that you like or agree with

YOU TRY IT!

1. Pick any book that you can easily find at home, open up to any page, and practice annotating as you read. If you shouldn't (or don't want to) write in your book, you can use sticky notes for your annotations instead of writing them on the book pages.

TEXT

2. Compare your annotations to the example of Bryce's annotation here:

more connection = more learning

When you are <u>studying for a test, you are strengthening the connections between neuron groups</u>. It makes sense that the <u>more connections you have, the more you will learn.</u> So when your friend suggested making index cards and testing one another, your brain was actively making more connections between the ideas and facts you were studying and strengthening the existing ones.

Active learning

Passive learning

<u>One of the best ways to make new strong connections is to think deeply about whatever it is you're studying.</u> That means you can't just read the text. That is quite (superficial) and will result in little, if any, learning. Instead, <u>try to create connections between the material you're studying and your own interests.</u> With your Civics exam, when you are trying to remember the <u>functions of each branch of the government</u>, think about how your school is a sort of mini-government. Your class is like a local government with the "laws" created and enforced by your teacher. Each class has a different local government. For example, your teacher may allow students to walk around during class, while another teacher may require everyone to stay seated. Your school is like a state government with the "laws" created and enforced by your principal and other administrative staff. For example, the school may decide that all students are required to wear uniforms, but not every school around you has this same rule. Your school district is like the federal government because it creates and enforces "laws" for all schools in the district to follow. For example, your school district decides when the first and last day of schools are for all the schools in your district, but not all schools in your state follow the same calendar. By <u>making the material more personal to you, you are creating stronger connections and will be more likely to remember the material for test time.</u>

?!

Ask Mr. Li
Aren't the "3 branches" the legislative, judicial, and executive?

PICK YOUR BRAIN

Love this! ☺

A (mnemonic device) is something people use to remember things. Neuroscience and medical students have to learn the names and order of the 12 cranial nerves (see Chapter 11) as part of their training. A popular mnemonic device for remembering all 12 goes like this: the **O**dor **O**f **O**rangutan **T**errified **T**arzan **A**fter **F**orty **V**oracious **G**orillas **V**iciously **A**ttacked **H**im. The first letter of each word is the same as the first letter of each cranial nerve, in order from one to 12: **O**lfactory, **O**ptic, **O**culomotor, **T**rochlear, **T**rigeminal, **A**bducens, **F**acial, **V**estibulocochlear, **G**lossopharyngeal, **V**agus, **A**ccessory, and **H**ypoglossal.

TAKING

TAKING NOTES involves rewriting or restating information in your own words on a separate piece of paper to help deepen your understanding and help you remember important details.

The most important pieces of information to include in notes are:

- the main idea
- any important details
- connections between events and concepts
- vocabulary terms
- key people, events, and dates

YOU TRY IT!

1. Read the following passage and take notes as you read. Give yourself a ten-minute time limit to thoroughly take notes.

2. After the ten minutes is up, compare your notes to the example of AJ's notes on the next page. (Don't peek yet—do the activity yourself first, and then check to see if you included all of the important information in your notes.)

NOTES

WHY SLEEP?

It seems like such a chore having to go to bed. You have to brush your teeth and change into your pjs just so you can waste a bunch of time lying down with your eyes closed not texting your friends or watching your favorite tv show. Well, even though it may seem as though you're doing nothing, your body is hard at work while you're sleeping! Scientists believe there are many reasons for why we sleep and one of them has to do with the fact that your body needs time to recoup, reorganize, and get ready for another day of active thinking and moving. While you're sleeping, your body is growing muscles, repairing tissues, and restoring hormone levels. Another very important thing that happens while we're sleeping is that your brain is solidifying all the information you learned during the day into your memory. Lots of experiments show that people are better able to remember things after a good night's sleep. Scientists think this is because the connections between neurons in your brain are strengthened while you sleep (see Chapter 6). This is why pulling an all-nighter before an exam is a bad idea. Without sleep, your brain can't encode all the information that you're studying into memory. You're better off getting sleep between studying and taking your trigonometry test!

SLEEP DEPRIVATION

Many people have trouble sleeping. Some have problems falling asleep and others have problems staying asleep. Both of these issues can lead to **sleep deprivation**. There are many negative consequences of sleep deprivation, including feeling overly emotional, being more sensitive to pain, hallucinating, and having poor concentration and memory. Randy Gardner was a high school student and in 1964, he remained awake for 11 days and 25 minutes (264.4 hours). Randy's attempt was closely watched by researchers who documented his physical and mental well-being throughout his entire time awake. As time went on, Randy became moody, paranoid, and started to hallucinate. He also was unable to concentrate, and his memory was poor. On the 11th day, he was asked to count backwards from 100 by 7s: 100...93...86...79...72...65. He just stopped at 65 and was silent. When asked why he stopped, he said he couldn't remember what he was doing! His memory and concentration had gotten so bad that he couldn't go on.

Sleep (pg. 52 Big Brain Book)

Why We Need Sleep

★ → body recoups, reorganizes + gets ready for next day
- muscle growth
- tissue repair
- restore hormones
- strengthens neuron connections to help you learn + remember info

Sleep Deprivation

★ → hard for many ppl to fall asleep or stay sleeping

★ → sleep deprivation = not enough sleep

★ → sleep deprivation is harmful bc
- more emotional, more sensitive to pain
- hallucinations
- trouble remembering + concentrating

ex. Randy Gardner research study
- HS student awake 264.4 hrs. (> 11 days)
- Sleep deprivation made him: moody, paranoid, hallucinate, unable to concentrate + remember

Bottom line → Our body + brain needs to sleep!
Too little sleep → sleep deprivation, which is harmful + causes moodiness, paranoid thoughts + hallucinations, and trouble concentrating.

How did your notes compare to AJ's? Were yours as thorough or detailed? Did it help to see what it looks like when you include the main idea and other details? Taking notes on what you read might seem pretty straightforward, but it can be hard to find the specific information you're looking for if you don't have a strategy. Tool #4 is a good strategy to help you get the most out of your notes.

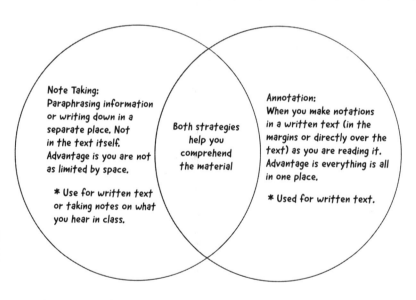

Note Taking:
Paraphrasing information or writing down in a separate place. Not in the text itself. Advantage is you are not as limited by space.

* Use for written text or taking notes on what you hear in class.

Both strategies help you comprehend the material

Annotation:
When you make notations in a written text (in the margins or directly over the text) as you are reading it. Advantage is everything is all in one place.

* Used for written text.

Annotating text and taking notes are similar, but they're done in different ways (one is right in the text and one is on a separate sheet of paper or note cards). There is no one right way for annotation and note taking, and you can use any symbols or systems that work for you. The way you do it doesn't matter as much as just doing it! As long as you include all relevant information, the exact style is up to you. Use what works for you based on your preferred learning style!

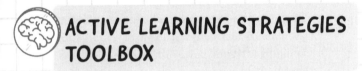

ACTIVE LEARNING STRATEGIES TOOLBOX

TOOL #1: MAKE AN ACTIVE READING BOOKMARK

Take an index card (note card) and write down the following questions:

- What stands out to me?
- Why is this part important?
- How does this connect to what I already know?
- Which vocabulary terms are new to me? Which parts of the word do I recognize?
- How would I summarize what I just read in a few sentences?
- What follow-up questions do I have?
- What makes me wonder?

Use the index card as a bookmark, and keep it with you as you're reading. Pause every so often (every few pages) to actively think about what you're reading (be metacognitive) by answering some of these questions. You can jot down your answers on small sticky notes and put the sticky note on the pages where you made those connections.

TOOL #2: USE YOUR VOICE

Record yourself saying the information that you're learning into a voice recorder or voice recording app, almost like you're the teacher explaining it. Later, listen to the recording. Speaking out loud helps to strengthen your storage of information in your memory, and listening to your voice helps you personalize the experience, both of which lead to better recollection later.

TOOL #3: PERFORM IT!

Sometimes, we remember what we do more easily than what we say. So acting it out is a kinesthetic strategy that many learners find helpful and enjoyable!

Read through the text or other information you are trying to learn, and act out what is happening as if you were an actor in a movie. As you do, try to link together what you're saying with the movements you're making. Focusing on the movements you make will help you remember the information. It may seem a bit silly, but sometimes being overly dramatic or loud, or even saying something in a funny voice, will help you remember the material better.

For example, if you're reading about George Washington crossing the Delaware River during the Revolutionary War, walk around the room, acting out the scene as if you were Washington. Make up what he might have said based on the facts given in the text, and use an exaggerated voice (which will make it easier to remember).

Sometimes the energy and delivery helps us remember, so pretending that you are teaching it to a class, giving a presentation, or even being a comedian or singer helps. If you make it fun for yourself, the information will be easier to recall later. When studying the elements for science, maybe you make up a rap about it and walk around the room rapping. No one else ever has to hear it—but we bet you'll remember it later!

TOOL #4 GET THE MOST OUT OF YOUR NOTES

Try these strategies to bump up your notes to the next level:

- Use a new page for each lesson or topic.

- Put the date and a title/label at the top of every page.

- Leave space in the margins and the last few lines on the page for adding in extra information later (because when you review your notes, you might find there's more information to add in).

- Use abbreviations and symbols when it makes sense, instead of writing everything out.

- Use bulleted phrases instead of full, complete sentences.

- Use a consistent color-coding system for your notes. There's evidence that color can help you recall information! But it has to be done right. Instead of highlighting everything you write, use color sparingly and with purpose to help you organize, focus on specific details, and stay motivated. As you review your notes, those highlighted things will be easier to find. For example, highlight:

- titles in pink;
- important people and dates in yellow;
- new vocabulary terms in blue; and
- definitions in green.

TOOL #5: USE ACRONYMS AND ACROSTICS

Acronyms and acrostics are "**mnemonic strategies**," which means they are tricks to help you remember complex information.

ACRONYMS are abbreviations built out of the first letter of other words. You can use acronyms to help you remember lists of items. For example, the acronym "HOMES" helps you remember the names of the Great Lakes (Huron, Ontario, Michigan, Erie, Superior).

ACROSTICS are sentences created using the first letters of the words in a list you're trying to remember. For example, the acrostic "My Very Educated Mother Just Served Us Nachos" is a silly sentence that helps you remember the order of the planets in our solar system (Mercury, Venus, Earth, Mars, Jupiter, Saturn, Uranus, and Neptune).

Try making up your own the next time you have to memorize a list of things for school.

Before we end this chapter, let's circle back to the different learning challenges we briefly mentioned in Chapter 5. We want to emphasize that everyone is different, and the learning strategies that work for one person will not be exactly the same as the strategies that work for someone else. We encourage you to try all of the tools we mentioned in the Toolbox, but we are not expecting that they will all work for you. You might need to tweak these tools to best fit your individual learning profile—and we encourage you to take ownership by doing that!

We hope this chapter has given you some new tools to add to your learning strategies and study skills toolbox. It might take some work to develop these strategies, but once you do, they'll become second nature and make learning flow much better.

IN THE NEXT CHAPTER, WE'LL TALK ABOUT SOME OF THE THINGS THAT GET IN THE WAY OF BEING PRODUCTIVE, EVEN WITH ACTIVE LEARNING STRATEGIES.

Chapter 7

Planning, Prioritizing, and Procrastination

Are you a member of the **SUCCESSFUL STUDENTS CLUB**?

~~Secret~~

Successful Students Club!

For Everyone!

Just kidding! There isn't actually a secret club for students that makes them successful, but it's easy to look around and feel like some kids seem to have school all figured out while you don't! There's no secret club, but there *are* certain strategies and actions (called "**EXECUTIVE FUNCTIONS**") that most successful students are using (whether they realize it or not!).

Executive functioning strategies help you learn new things, remember information, and make connections. We use executive functions for everything we do...from getting ready for school, to doing homework, to planning an afternoon at the movies with friends.

Think about the people you can count on in your life—the people who are always on time, always do what they say they will, get a lot accomplished, and learn from their mistakes. They don't have a magic wand or even luck—they're using executive functioning strategies. In this chapter, we'll show you a few of these mental skills that are extra helpful for school success: organization, planning, prioritizing tasks, and self-monitoring.

SCHOOL SUCCESS BEGINS WITH GOOD ORGANIZATION SKILLS!

Quiz

How organized are you when it comes to completing your assignments? Grab a piece of paper and a pencil and take this self-quiz to find out. Number your paper from 1 to 14, then give yourself an honest rating for each question, where *no* is 1 point, *sometimes* is 2, and *yes* is 3.

1. Do you have a regular place where you study/work?

2. Do you have a specific time of day that you study and do your homework each day?

3. Do you study/do your homework without a lot of distractions (like your cell phone, tablet, TV, etc.)?

4. Do you bring everything you need to school and home each day (books, papers, permission slips, homework, etc.)?

5. Is it easy for you to find all of your stuff (earphones, books, sports equipment, etc.)?

6. Can you easily find papers that you are looking for (at home or in locker)?

7. Would other people say your desk or workspace at home is neat and organized?

8. Do you have a system for keeping track of your grades in each of your classes?

9. Do you have a system for keeping track of assignments and due dates that you look at daily?

10. Do you have a good system for finding out what you have for homework when you are absent?

11. Do you have a good system for getting material that you miss when you are absent (like class notes, handouts, homework, etc.)?

12. Do you start each assignment by reading (or rereading) the directions?

13. Do you double-check your work to make sure it is done correctly and completely before turning it in?

14. Do you complete and turn in your assignments on time?

Add up your scores. If your overall total is less than 36, adding some new tools to your current organizational system will make a big difference! Which areas of organization are you strong in? Which could use help from a few more strategies?

If you have a high score on questions #8–11 because you use an online school portal, do you have a backup plan in case you're not able to access the portal or your teacher doesn't post information promptly?

Why is being organized so important?

Because it actually helps you get things done quicker! Plus, it's a good habit to get into before high school, where you'll have even *more* to keep track of.

Take a look at what the crew has learned about their organizational habits and systems. They each made minor changes to the way they managed their time, space, and actions to give themselves additional structure, and those small changes have made a significant impact on their schoolwork.

- Maddie used to do her homework while she watched TV, and realized that she didn't remember the information very well, and sometimes didn't do everything she was supposed to. So she started doing her homework in a place free from a lot of distractions. Now she's getting her homework done faster, and understanding it better—and she still has time for TV (without the distraction of homework!) after.

- Carlo didn't use to plan a specific time to do his homework, and sometimes didn't finish it all before he had to go to bed. So he tried making a homework schedule for a specific time of day when he felt most productive. For example, he knows he needs to take a few minutes when he first gets home to have a snack and relax a little bit, then get started on his homework to get it all finished.

- Dillon used to turn in a lot of assignments late, which lowered his grade and made his parents and teachers (and him!) frustrated. So he started writing down all of his assignments in his assignment book every day to keep track of what was due, even if he thought he would remember it. Now he feels much more in control.

- Bryce used to feel stressed trying to fit in all of her after-school obligations and homework. So she made a calendar system to keep track of everything, which helps her plan out and prepare for each day.

- AJ used to feel angry because they could never find what they were looking for easily. So they started using an organizational system for their notebook. They organized it with sections for different classes, and kept things in order from newest to oldest. Writing the date and a heading on the top of each paper also helps them find what they're looking for quickly.

Take a Minute!

Can you think of any small, easy changes you could make to...

- **ORGANIZE YOUR THINGS DIFFERENTLY** to have a more productive study space and be able to find your materials more easily?

- Be better able to **KEEP TRACK** of all of your assignments?

- **REMEMBER YOUR SCHEDULE** so you get your assignments in on time?

It could be as simple as actually using the planner that is sitting there empty, or getting a couple of shelves or drawers at home to organize school materials.

YOU'VE GOT TO HAVE A PLAN

Remember the quote from Chapter 2: "A goal without a plan is just a wish"? Well, it's true: a plan is necessary for reaching your goals. Your goal is where you want to end up. Your plan is the path to get you there—what you will do, how you will do it, when you will do it, and how long you think it will take you.

It's important to have a plan before you start because there's never only one way to make something happen. You need to decide the best way for *you* to get it done—because the plan that works best for you may not be the same as the plan that works for someone else.

Part of the planning process includes *time management*, which is knowing about how long something will take, and using that information in your plan so you can finish when you need to.

Let's talk more about why planning and time management are important. Does this situation sound familiar to you?

The Main Street Middle School science fair was coming up, and all students were required to do a project as part of their science grade. The teacher announced that everyone had to choose a topic to investigate, create a hypothesis, conduct an experiment, write up the results, and then bring a poster to school on science fair day showing the results.

Without time management and planning, due dates can sneak up on you, and before you know what's happened, you realize that you have very little time and a lot of work to do. Take a look at the time management and planning challenges that the crew had with the science fair.

- AJ and their parents had somewhere to go, and AJ told them, "I'll be done in 10 minutes," but it was 30 minutes before they were finished, and their parents were frustrated.

- Bryce wanted to get all of her research done before band practice. But, she only finished half of what she wanted to read before she had to leave.

- Maddie didn't think it would take very long and didn't thoroughly think through everything she had to do, so she didn't start on her poster until the day before it was due and had to rush to get everything done. As a result, her grade was not as high as it could have been if she had made a plan.

- Carlo asked his mom to drop him off at the library to get the books he needed to research his topic and told his mom to pick him up in two hours. But it ended up only taking him 25 minutes to find what he needed, and he had a long time to wait for her to pick him up.

- Dillon quickly came up with a topic that he was excited about and knew what he wanted the end result to be, but he didn't make a plan for each step and assumed he could wait to start until two days before it was due.

As you can see, the crew had some challenges with managing their time. As a result, Bryce, Maddie, and Dillon didn't finish everything on time, and AJ and Carlo's parents were frustrated. If they had managed their time a little more accurately, they could have avoided that unnecessary stress.

If you are like the crew and estimating the amount of time that tasks take isn't something that comes naturally to you, this exercise can help you close the gap between your estimates and the actual time that something takes you to complete.

Grab a pen! ✏️

Step 1. On a piece of paper, draw and label four columns, like Maddie's example on the next page.

Step 2. Write a task you need to complete and estimate the amount of time you think it will take you (be as specific as possible with what you need to do).

Step 3. Time yourself doing the task, from start to finish. Don't forget to include the time it takes you to get your supplies together! Keep the timer going until you have completed the task thoroughly. Record the actual time it took.

Step 4. Reflect on the differences between your estimate and reality. Why were there differences between your estimated time and the actual time it took? What took longer or shorter? What would change in your estimate of a similar task next time?

TASK (BE SPECIFIC)	ESTIMATED TIME TO COMPLETE	ACTUAL TIME TO COMPLETE	REFLECTION: WERE THERE DIFFERENCES BETWEEN ESTIMATE AND ACTUAL TIME? WHY?
Complete sections 2 and 3 on math study guide	20 minutes	48 minutes	Finding my calculator took me a few minutes and I had to go sharpen my pencil. Then, when I got to the problems in section 3, I didn't remember how to do those kinds of problems so I had to look back through my notes to find examples and that took me a while.

We suggest that you do this activity a few times, with different types of tasks. Be your own detective as you reflect on what caused you to take more (or less) time than your estimate. As you practice, you will make progress toward more accurate time estimates. Once you have an accurate idea of how long different kinds of tasks take you, you'll be able to confidently plan other activities in your daily schedule without worrying that you won't have enough time for your schoolwork.

Here are some ideas of ways you can plan out your work and activities:

- Fill out a **GRAPHIC ORGANIZER** before you start writing an essay

- Keep a **CALENDAR** of your extracurricular activities and social activities

- **SEPARATE THE STEPS** in a long-term project and do a little bit at a time
- Decide what **OPERATIONS OR PROCEDURES** to use for a math word problem
- Determine what (and how) **TO STUDY** for an upcoming test
- **PACK YOUR BACKPACK** and lay out your clothes for the next day before you go to bed

CAN YOU THINK OF ANY OTHER WAYS YOU PLAN?

Everyone has the ability to plan, though people do it in different ways, and planning comes more naturally to some people. Even if planning doesn't come naturally to you, with intention and practice, your brain can adapt and grow and get better (this is called "neuroplasticity").

Before starting an assignment, identify your goal and how you want the final product to look. Read the directions and maybe even re-write them, to make sure you know all the details and guidelines you need to follow. Make a list of the materials you will need for each step. Then plan out a timeline for when you will do each step and estimate the time it will take.

PLANNING BEFORE YOU BEGIN WILL HELP YOU FEEL CONFIDENT AND MOTIVATED, AND WILL ALSO MAKE GETTING STARTED EASIER!

PRIORITIZING (AND *NOT* PROCRASTINATING)

Now that you know that planning involves creating a roadmap for yourself and managing your time, the next step is to **prioritize.** Prioritizing means deciding which tasks are most important at each step along the path to reaching your goals. To prioritize, you need to know what's most important for your short-term and long-term goals. For example, doing your math homework before playing basketball because you want to get a good grade in the class.

Think back to the changes the crew made to organize their time. Maddie, Carlo, and AJ practiced prioritizing as a part of their plan. Maddie prioritized doing well on her homework over watching TV. Carlo prioritized his schoolwork over social activities. AJ prioritized learning to be organized over finishing their work quickly.

The more activities you're involved in, the more essential it is to prioritize—because no one can do it all. Prioritizing doesn't mean never getting to have fun! It means thinking about what is most important to you—not just in the moment, but also in the long term, and making responsible choices.

REALITY CHECK! It happens to you. It happens to us. It happens to everyone, sometimes...that nagging thought about what you *should* be doing that you push to the back of your mind because you just don't feel like doing it. That's called **procrastination.** It's easy to avoid tasks that are challenging, time-consuming, or not particularly interesting to you. It probably feels comfortable in the moment to avoid them or choose something more fun instead, but in the long term, it doesn't help you reach your goals. In fact, procrastination often leads to things piling up, which can cause you even more stress.

Many times, students wait to feel motivated before they start their work, which leads to procrastination... because usually, we don't get suddenly motivated to do hard things out of the blue! The trick is, if you just make yourself get started, *then* you will usually get a burst of motivation to complete the task. So **ACTION** comes first, then motivation. Think of the Nike saying **JUST DO IT!**

Take a Minute!

Do any of these thoughts sound like you?

- It's hard for me to make myself sit down and do my homework or study, so I put off studying or don't study at all.

- I take breaks from homework or studying that are probably too frequent or too long.

- I have difficulty setting aside fun activities to start homework or chores and often need reminders to get started.

- I have trouble sticking with homework or studying long enough to do it well enough to get the score I really want.

- It's hard for me to decide what to do first when I have a lot of things to do. Like when I have a big project, I'm not sure what to do first, what the parts are, what to do next, etc.

- I often feel overwhelmed by long-term projects or big assignments unless someone is there to help me.

If these sound familiar, you might struggle with prioritization and tend to procrastinate. But that's okay! We're here to help.

REMEMBER, THE PROCESS IS JUST AS IMPORTANT (IF NOT MORE IMPORTANT) AS THE PRODUCT, AND FOCUSING ON YOUR GOALS IS THE KEY TO DEVELOPING AN ACTION PLAN, PRACTICING GRIT, AND HAVING A GROWTH MINDSET.

SELF-MONITORING (AND SELF-EVALUATION)

You've made a plan, but now how do you know if it's a good plan? As we've said, there isn't only one way or one best way for everyone to learn, motivate themselves, or make plans. But there *is* a best way to know if the plan you made is working: give it a try and see how it goes! Yep, it's as simple as that. As you work, be your own detective. Pause every so often to be metacognitive—check in with yourself to see if you're staying focused on the task or getting distracted (this is called **SELF-MONITORING**) and think about the progress you are making (this is called **SELF-EVALUATION**). Those metacognitive check-ins help you know if your plan is working, and if it isn't, you can adjust your plan to get you closer to reaching your goal.

IT'S OK IF YOUR PLANS DON'T ALWAYS WORK PERFECTLY—THAT'S PART OF THE LEARNING PROCESS.

REALITY CHECK! For some people, it takes more time and practice to build good executive functioning strategies, especially if they also have difficulty with regulating their attention or learning easily. But if you're one of those people, using executive functioning strategies is even more crucial for your success! Use the tools in the toolbox on the next pages and remember the mantra, **PRACTICE MAKES PROGRESS!**

EXECUTIVE FUNCTIONING TOOLBOX

TOOL #1: USE A 3-PART CALENDAR SYSTEM TO INCREASE YOUR PRODUCTIVITY AND ORGANIZATION

Part 1: A monthly calendar

A monthly calendar gives you the big picture of what's coming up in your school and personal life. Write all of your extracurricular activities, family obligations, and big project due dates on your monthly calendar so that with a quick glance you can see how everything fits together and when you have a lot going on around the same time. When you find out about a due date or event, add it into your monthly calendar.

January

Sun	Mon	Tue	Wed	Thu	Fri	Sat
1	2	③ mom's b-day!	④ back to school	5	6	7
8	9	10	11	12	13	14
15	⑯ MLK day no school	17	18	19	20	21
22	23	24	25	26	27	28
29	30	㉛ momma's b-day!				

Part 2: A weekly task list

A weekly schedule helps you think about what you have to do not just today, but for a span of a few days in a row. Weekly plans are especially helpful if you have a lot of obligations after school that you have to plan other things (like homework) around, or if you have teachers who give some assignments that are not due the next day (they're due in a few days, or a week). At the beginning of each week, make a weekly schedule that includes assignments that are due, social events, after-school activities, and family obligations for that week.

Monday	Tuesday	
Band Practice	Math test	
Wednesday	Thursday	
Band Practice	Essay due	
Friday	Sat	Sun
Movie night with friends		

Part 3: A daily to-do list

A daily to-do list is important because out of sight is often out of mind. Each day, make a list of things you need to accomplish that day, including school assignments, family obligations, and social activities. Refer to your list often and cross off each item as you complete it. Crossing things off your list can be surprisingly satisfying!

Monday

Math — finish study guide

Science — read article and annotate

English — rough draft of essay

Band practice 3– 5

TOOL #2: PRIORITIZE BY IMMEDIACY AND IMPORTANCE

Sometimes it's hard to know what to start with when you have a lot to do. This tool will help you prioritize by considering the importance and urgency of the things on your weekly task list.

Start by making yourself a graphic organizer like the one here. Then go through your weekly task list and write each item from your list in one of the four sections based on how important it is and how quickly it needs to be done.

	VERY IMPORTANT	NOT AS IMPORTANT
IMMEDIATE	* math test tomorrow worth 50 points	* science homework due tomorrow worth 5 points
NOT AS IMMEDIATE	* essay draft for ELA due in two weeks	* take photos for next month's photo club meeting

Seems simple, but sometimes just taking a minute to acknowledge which things are most important and urgent can really help you get started!

TOOL #3: MAKE A PLAN

Making a plan actually helps to motivate us to start and to keep going even if the task is challenging (or we aren't interested in it). It helps you think it through before you begin, so you're mindful about your specific goal and have a roadmap for how to get there. Check out Maddie's plan for getting math homework done for some good questions to ask yourself while you're making a plan.

WHAT IS MY SPECIFIC GOAL?	I have to finish my math homework (30 mixed review problems) before I have to go to soccer practice.
WHERE SHOULD I START?	I want to start with an easy one.
HOW SHOULD I PROCEED?	I will do the easy ones first, then move on to the more difficult ones because I will feel less overwhelmed as I get some done.
WHAT STRATEGIES COULD I USE TO HELP ME REACH THE GOAL?	I could simplify first, look for patterns, and color-code based on which operation I have to use.

Remember the active and passive learning strategies from Chapter 6? Make sure to keep the difference between active and passive learning in mind! Your plans are always going to be more productive in the end if you use active learning strategies, even if they take more effort. Remember that organization, planning, prioritizing tasks, and metacognition take practice—but it's definitely worth the effort!

SEE YOU IN CHAPTER 8, MANAGING YOUR STRESS!

Chapter 8

Managing Your Stress

$\mathcal{W}$elcome to Chapter 8: Managing Your Stress. **EVERYONE GETS STRESSED**—it's just part of life! But if you can learn to recognize when you feel stressed, and the patterns it usually comes in, you can stop it from becoming overwhelming. If you've read the chapters of this book in order so far, you've probably figured out that a lot of the journey through middle school is about learning more about yourself—so let's get started learning about stress.

Bryce has a lot going on!

Have you ever felt like this?

You may not have had exactly the same things going on, but you've probably had similar feelings when you had a lot to do. So what is stress, and why do we experience it?

 ## What is stress?

Stress is the body's response to life situations that cause feelings of tremendous pressure, or that seem overwhelming, upsetting, or threatening. And we all have those sometimes! Stress comes in many shapes and sizes, and can even be helpful. For example, having a due date or a time limit can motivate you to get working! But there can be times when you feel too much stress, and when this happens, it may cause you to avoid things you need to get done. We like to think of it as a meter than can range from low stress to high stress, and with each level, your productivity is influenced or affected.

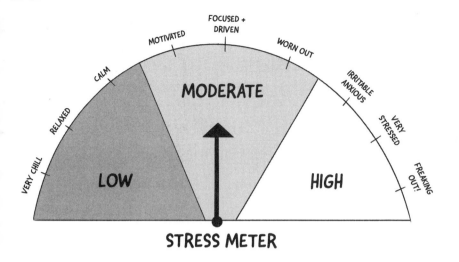

STRESS METER

There can be a lot of stressful parts of middle school!
Here are common ones:

Busy schedule

Extra-curriculars

Homework

Test anxiety

Grades

Peer pressure

Parent pressure

Social media

Friend drama

THE BODY'S RESPONSE TO STRESS

Imagine a cave person, living millions of years ago, who left her home to hunt for food and gather supplies... when suddenly she was confronted by a saber-tooth tiger twice her size, snarling with massive teeth and large claws, ready to pounce! She had three options to choose from:

1. **FIGHT** the tiger,

2. **FLIGHT**—run as fast as she could, or

3. **FREEZE** and hope it loses interest and leaves.

These reactions are controlled by our brain and nervous system.

When confronted with a stressful situation, here's what happens inside your body. First, your brain receives the information (the stressful event), and specific parts of the brain (the amygdala and hypothalamus) are activated, which sets off an alarm system to your body that says "threat, danger, discomfort, fear!" The "danger" message travels throughout our body through hormones and chemicals (such as adrenaline and cortisol) that activate the **SYMPATHETIC** and **PARASYMPATHETIC NERVOUS SYSTEMS,** which control our body's response to stressful situations.

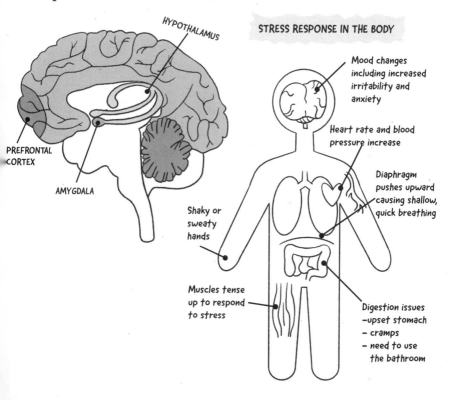

HYPOTHALAMUS

PREFRONTAL CORTEX

AMYGDALA

STRESS RESPONSE IN THE BODY

Mood changes including increased irritability and anxiety

Heart rate and blood pressure increase

Diaphragm pushes upward causing shallow, quick breathing

Shaky or sweaty hands

Muscles tense up to respond to stress

Digestion issues
–upset stomach
– cramps
– need to use the bathroom

Even after millions of years, our brains still respond similarly when we encounter a stressful situation. Obviously, Bryce's stress at the beginning of the chapter is not the same as facing a saber tooth tiger, but her brain and body are having a fight, flight, or freeze response, just like the cavewoman. Her heart might be pounding, her palms might be sweating, and her muscles might be tense. She might also be thinking, "What do I do? How can I possibly get this all done?" The physical reactions, thoughts, and feelings we experience influence how we react to stress.

Regardless of what you perceive as stressful, your body will respond the same way. It's important to know both your most common stressors, *and* how your body and mind respond to them. What's stressful to one person might not be stressful to another!

HOW STRESS PRESENTS IN YOU

Here's a list of common reactions (**BODY, THOUGHTS, AND BEHAVIORS**) that people have when they feel stressed. Do any of these sound familiar? How often do you have reactions like these? Make a list of some of your common ones—this can help you learn to recognize when you're starting to get stressed.

PHYSICAL (BODY)

Low energy or feeling restless

Racing heart

Chest pain

Hard to breathe

Headache/migraines

Muscle tension

Shaky in legs, arms or whole body

Upset stomach

Dry mouth

Clenched jaw or grinding teeth

Loss of appetite or eating a lot

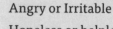

THOUGHTS/FEELINGS

Worrying

Angry or Irritable

Hopeless or helpless

Sadness

Thinking Errors (Chapter 3)

- Catastrophizing
- All or Nothing Thinking
- Filtering
- Shoulds
- Overgeneralizing

Feeling impatient

Feeling powerless

Feeling overcommitted

Fixed mindset

BEHAVIORS

Snapping at family and others

Not paying attention in class or skipping class

Treating friends poorly

Avoiding responsibilities

Procrastinating

Comparing yourself to others or gossiping

Anxious behaviors (nail biting, skin picking, fidgeting, etc.)

Spending excessive time on social media

Experimenting with drugs and alcohol

Worrying too much and assuming everything will go wrong

Trying to be perfect

I always get an upset stomach and feel shaky. Sometimes I clench my jaw.

I start to get tense muscles and the next thing I know I'm snapping at my friends and family.

The key to dealing with stressors like these is to activate the *thinking* part of the brain rather than the *reacting* part of the brain (which was trying to get you to fight, freeze, or flee). The thinking part of the brain is called the prefrontal cortex, and controls planning, organization, impulses, and attention (just to name a few). When we get the prefrontal cortex involved, we can react to stressful situations more effectively, rather than just using our instincts. For those of you wondering about the cavewoman, after her brain sent out the "DANGER" message, she initially froze but then locked eyes with the tiger, pulled out the food she had gathered, and tossed it. The tiger ran after the food, and she ran home to her cave, safe and sound!

SELF-CARE AND COPING STRATEGIES

So now that you have a better understanding of stress, it's time to do something about it! One way to keep your stress level balanced is through **SELF-CARE**. Self-care involves daily practices and routines that help the stress meter sit comfortably between low and moderate stress. Sometimes the daily self-care practices aren't enough to help you when your stress is getting high or has spiked over to the freaking out range! When that happens, it's time to try some coping skills—which can actually be similar to self-care.

TAKING AN ACTIVE ROLE IN YOUR WELL-BEING IS LIKE TAKING AN ACTIVE ROLE AS A LEARNER. IT MAY FEEL LIKE MORE WORK AT THE BEGINNING, BUT IT'S WORTH IT IN THE LONG RUN!

SELF-CARE

There are endless practices that can be considered part of self-care, and you will have your own that are not on this list. We've grouped them into five categories: sleep/rest, exercise/movement, social/cultural, mindfulness, and nutrition/hygiene.

Take a look at the list on the next page—which do you do?

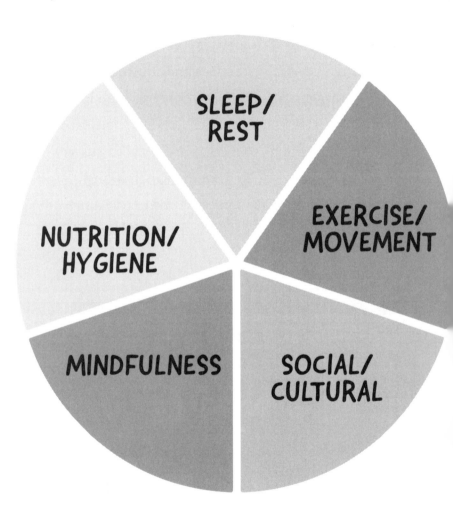

SLEEP/REST

- Do you get 9 to 12 hours of sleep each night?

- Do you go to bed and wake up at around the same time every day?

- Do you give your body time to rest and relax when you're not sleeping?

EXERCISE/MOVEMENT

- Do you make time for movement (like stretching or walking) every day?

- Do you engage in 30-60 minutes of physical exercise most days?

- Do you play sports?

SOCIAL/CULTURAL

- Do you have family, friends, or others you can talk to that you trust?

- Do you make time to interact with these people weekly?

- Do you have access to support groups based on your cultural preferences?

- Do you make time to laugh with friends and family?

- Do you make time for your spiritual practices, if that's something important to you?

MINDFULNESS

- Do you make time to be fully present in the moment?

- Do you find time to rest your mind by taking a break from school, activities, and technology?

NUTRITION/HYGIENE

- Do you eat a variety of nutritious foods (fruits, vegetables, proteins, grains) instead of going straight for sweets, fried foods, or caffeine?

- Do you drink at least 8 cups (64 ounces) of water a day?

- Do you shower daily?

- Do you wear clean clothes?

- Do you use deodorant?

We don't expect you to do all of these, and the number you do can also be impacted by your current stress level or other factors. For example, if you're reading this book during the school year, you might feel a different stress level than if you're reading it during your summer break. Take a closer look at your responses—are there any groups where you don't do *any*? If so, consider adding simple changes to your routine to promote more self-care.

COPING SKILLS

To use healthy coping skills, you need to listen to your body and know what you need to feel better when things are tough. Just like your preferred learning style is unique to you, the coping skills also have to be the right fit. Developing effective coping skills takes practice and willingness to try new strategies.

Sometimes people unintentionally develop unhealthy coping skills. Unhealthy coping skills are things that lessen stress in the short term but can have long-term negative consequences. Many of the stressed behaviors from the chart on page 213 are examples of unhealthy coping (procrastinating, using drugs and alcohol, snapping at friends and family, etc.). Try to catch yourself if you use those unhealthy strategies and replace them with some of these more effective skills:

BEHAVIORS OR ACTIONS TO ADDRESS THE PHYSICAL (BODY)	BEHAVIORS OR ACTIONS TO ADDRESS THE THOUGHTS/ FEELINGS

• Short high-intensity exercise
  • Jumping jacks
  • Push-up
  • Squats
  • Sprint for 1 minute
  • Lift weights
 	
• Longer less intense exercise
  • Go for a run or walk
  • Play a sport
  • Yoga and relaxed stretching
 	
• Progressive muscle relaxation
• Calm breathing
• Sing a song you like as loud as you can
• Have a snack that nourishes you
• Drink water
• Take a shower
	• Give yourself permission to feel
	• Practice positive or neutral statements of encouragement (activating your growth mindset)
	• Write out your worries—give them a new place to be other than in your brain
	• Problem-solve with someone you trust
	• Talk to a friend for fun
	• Time management strategies from Chapter 7
	• Watch a funny video
	• Look at pleasant images
	• Guided or self-directed meditation
	• Guided imagery of your favorite place
	• Mindfulness
	• Baking or cooking
	• Making something creative—drawing, sewing, coloring

Maddie engages in proactive self-care by exercising every day and drinking two full bottles of water. She also listens to a 10-minute meditation before bed several nights a week. If she becomes tense and has negative self-talk while doing math homework, she uses her coping skills by reviewing her positive self-talk cards and practicing deep-breathing exercises.

Carlo practices self-care by staying extremely connected with his family. He makes a point to text his grandpa often, and participates in weekly Saturday family dinners. He also attends weekly youth group activities to hang out with friends. When stressed about schoolwork, he likes to take a quick drawing break and listen to music.

Coping skills are meant to be enjoyable—the whole point is that they relax you! So give self-care a try. We bet you'll like it! Check out the toolbox for some of our favorite coping tools.

 SELF-CARE TOOL BOX

TOOL #1: DEEP BREATHING VS. "JUST BREATHING"

You've probably had adults in your life tell you to "just breathe" when you're stressed, and you may have heard it so often that now you're annoyed by it. We hear lots of kids say, "Ugh! I already breathe all day! Why do they suggest that?" Fair! But the difference is in breathing deeply, and a lot of people haven't been taught how and why to do that.

Here's why deep breathing is so helpful. Unlike the breathing that you do all day, without even thinking, deep breathing involves your conscious effort to allow the air to travel slowly and deeply, using your diaphragm and expanding your belly. This opens your lungs, slows down your heart rate, relaxes your muscles, and provides nourishing oxygen to your brain. Just the act of paying attention to your breathing gives you something else to focus on, other than the stress. Here are some ways to do it:

1. **ONE-NOSTRIL BREATHING**

   - While sitting or lying down, close one of your nostrils with your finger and close your mouth. Slowly breathe in through *only* your other nostril (keeping your mouth closed) and count to 5, then breathe out (still through the same nostril) for 7 counts. With practice, work your way up to a count of 8 to 10 in and 10 to 12 out.

   - Imagine your breath going down deep into your lungs and filling up your belly. Try setting a timer for two minutes, and work your way up to five minutes.

2. RECTANGLE BREATHING

- Place your hands on your lap or your belly. Imagine a rectangle (or look at a piece of notebook paper or even the back of your cell phone to avoid distractions).

- Imagine a dot that is going around the edge of the rectangle to help pace your breathing. With your mouth closed, look at the top left corner of the rectangle and breath in through your nose to the count of 4, imagining the dot moving across the top line.

- As you imagine the dot turning the corner of the rectangle and going down the side, exhale out of your mouth (slowly and deeply) to the count of 6.

- Repeat on the following two sides: breathe in on the bottom line, and out on the last side. Try setting a timer for one minute or going around the rectangle three times.

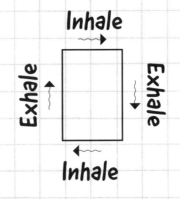

THE MOST IMPORTANT INSTRUCTION FOR ALL BREATHING STRATEGIES IS TO PRACTICE THE SKILL WHEN YOU'RE CALM SO THAT IT'S EASY TO DO WHEN YOU'RE STRESSED.

TOOL #2 PROGRESSIVE MUSCLE RELAXATION

Progressive Muscle Relaxation (PMR) involves tensing and relaxing specific groups of muscles. The point is to purposely create tension in the body so that you can experience an immediate sense of relaxation. Hopefully, as you feel each muscle relax, you can disconnect from the stressful thoughts and feelings. If you are someone who clenches your fists or jaw, grinds your teeth, locks your knees while standing, and tenses your neck and shoulders, this is for you! Follow these steps (it really helps to do them all, but even a quick tense and release of one muscle group can be helpful in a pinch!):

1. **Face:** Clench your jaw, press your lips tightly together, wrinkle your forehead down, and close your eyes as tightly as you can. Hold for 10 seconds, then release.

2. **Hands:** Clench them tight, like you're squeezing all the juice out of a lemon! Hold for 10 seconds and release.

3. **Wrists and forearms:** Stretch your arms out in front of you like you're pushing something away with your palms facing out (hold for 10 and release), then bend your wrists down so that your fingers point back toward you. Imagine your fingers could touch your forearm (hold for 10 and release).

4. **Biceps and shoulders:** Clench your fists and pull your arms close to the sides of your body like you're doing a super tight bicep curl. Squeeze your arms into the sides of your ribcage and tighten your shoulders up and in towards your ears. Hold for 10 and release.

5. **Back:** Push your chest toward the sky, clasp your hands behind your back, and allow your shoulders to roll back and your back to arch. Imagine you can make your elbows touch. Hold for 10 and release.

6. **Stomach:** Suck your belly in tight, like your belly button feels like it could touch your spine! Hold for 10 and release.

7. **Buttocks:** Squeeze your buttocks together as tight as you can. Hold for 10 and release.

8. **Legs:** While sitting upright, stretch your legs out in front of you. Point your toes up and slightly back toward you, allowing your calves and front of the legs to tighten. Hold for 10 and release.

9. **Whole Body:** Now, try tightening up your entire body. Starting with your face, then adding each part of the body. Imagine your entire body stiff as a board, holding for 10 seconds, and releasing, so you are as loose as a spaghetti noodle!

TOOL #3 MINDFULNESS

Being mindful involves being fully present in the current moment. For example, you can try being fully present right now as you look away from this book to notice what is around you. Where are you reading this book? Are you sitting or lying down? Are you comfortable? Is there a lamp on, or are you relying on natural sunlight? What do you hear—nature (birds, insects, the wind), cars driving by, a TV in another room, a buzzing fan, or even a chime or buzz alerting you to a notification on your phone? Do you feel hot or cold? Do you smell anything? Set a timer for one minute and give this a try.

Time's up! What did you notice? Did things come to your attention that you hadn't noticed before?

Did you encounter thoughts or other distractions? If you did, that's okay! Being mindful means noticing and accepting without judgment, and that includes your thoughts. By avoiding judgment or criticism of yourself, your thoughts, and things or people around you, you can begin to be fully present with a sense of peace.

Life can be hectic, with so many things distracting us from just being in our bodies and in a calm mind. Many people are not used to noticing the here and now and truly being in the moment. It can be hard to suddenly stop the fast-paced life full of distractions and just notice. Like the breathing strategies, it's important to practice this skill when you're calm so you can easily use it when stressed.

Practice with a specific activity.

Try to engage all of your senses and try to keep your attention on what you are doing right now. Think about what you feel, taste, smell, hear, and see in the moment. Here are a few examples to get you started. Start easy—try activities you find simple first.

- Drinking hot chocolate

- Eating a snack

- Getting dressed

- Taking a shower

- Doing a puzzle or sudoku

- Coloring or doing something creative

You can also try this experiment: eat a chocolate kiss quickly by chewing it. Then eat another chocolate kiss, but this time let it melt in your mouth without chewing it at all. As it melts, notice how different it tastes and feels. Is it creamier? Can you smell the chocolate more? Taste it more? Are the flavors more intense?

Give yourself gentle friendly reminders.

- For example, while working on a homework assignment, write on a post-it something like "Right now, I am focusing on my math homework." That way as your eyes wander you can read the note as a kind reminder to stay present.

- If you get stressed about your work, remind yourself, "I just need to take one step at a time and it will all get done."

Try Guided Meditations

Meditations are a form of mindfulness. Guided meditations are those where another person is telling you want to do or focus on (either in person, or by video/audio). There are many resources available, including apps and videos (just search "guided meditation"). Here are a few apps that we recommend:

- Insight Timer
- Calm
- Smiling Mind

We hope you begin to practice recognizing your stress and trying new self-care and coping skills. How stress affects your body is different for each person and each situation. For many people, once they add self-care strategies and the stressful event passes, relief kicks in. But sometimes people feel stressed constantly, and continue to feel stressed long after the stressor is gone. They may be experiencing something else, such as anxiety or depression. If you feel like your stress is out of control, or like you can't cope on your own, ask for help from a trusted adult.

IN THIS CHAPTER, WE'VE PROVIDED AN INTRODUCTION TO STRESS—BUT THERE'S MUCH MORE TO IT! IF YOU FOUND THIS CHAPTER HELPFUL AND WANT TO LEARN MORE, WE HIGHLY RECOMMEND READING ANOTHER BOOK IN THE KID CONFIDENT SERIES: *HOW TO HANDLE STRESS FOR MIDDLE SCHOOL SUCCESS* BY DR. SILVI GUERRA!

We've talked about what stress is, how it presents itself, and ways you can cope and practice self-care. In the next chapter, we talk about how you can use what you've learned to understand and advocate for what you need.

Chapter 9

Tying It All Together and Self-Determination

Welcome to Chapter 9, where we're going to bring all the previous chapters together. So far, we've looked at **WAYS OF THINKING** (mindset, grit, and motivation) and **WAYS OF IMPROVING YOUR SCHOOL EXPERIENCE** (navigating your environment, study strategies, and stress management). In this last chapter, we will show you **HOW YOUR THOUGHTS AND BEHAVIORS ARE CONNECTED, HOW YOUR THINKING AFFECTS YOUR ACTIONS,** and **HOW YOU CAN GROW YOUR SELF-DETERMINATION**. Let's get started!

The parts of navigating middle school that we discussed in Chapters 1–8 are really all about developing **SELF-DETERMINATION**. Basically, self-determination means making choices for yourself and feeling like you're in control of your own life! Being and feeling self-determined is important as you move through middle school, becoming more independent and making more decisions for yourself about your learning. **MOTIVATION, SELF-EFFICACY, MINDSET, GOAL SETTING, AND GRIT ALL FEED INTO BEING SELF-DETERMINED.** Self-determination is a big part of being successful!

Being self-determined helps you make decisions. Decision-making involves both **SELF-AWARENESS** (knowing what you need and why you need it) and **SELF-ADVOCACY** (knowing how to get what you need). Let's take a closer look...

SELF-AWARENESS

SELF-AWARENESS IS ABOUT UNDERSTANDING YOUR FEELINGS, MOTIVES, AND DESIRES, AND HOW THEY AFFECT WHY YOU CHOOSE TO DO THINGS. Middle school is the perfect time to become more aware of how you think, what you like and don't like, and what you want your character to be as you grow into an adult. In fact, part of your "job" as an adolescent is to figure out who you are—and to do that, you need self-awareness!

Take a look at Carlo's self-reflection on his strengths and challenges. Notice anything? He thought about a lot of the concepts we've talked about in this book, from mindfulness to coping with stress.

There are 5 kids in my family, and I'm the second oldest. At school, I love art but don't love English class. Understanding math comes pretty easily to me, but reading books and writing essays is hard. I have a great imagination and this year I've used it to help me by creating drawings and images in my mind while I read and when I have to do word problems in math. I really really want to get good grades, but a lot of the time it takes me forever to get my homework assignments done. There are lots of things going on at home and my brothers and sister (and two dogs and a guinea pig!) are pretty noisy, which makes it hard for me to concentrate sometimes.

When I'm doing something I like, like art, I usually have a growth mindset and tons of grit and motivation. I know that with practice, I will get better and I know that I need to practice to get better, so I look for ways to get that practice and improve my art skills. I watch videos and like trying out different techniques. I even try to use art for things that are hard for me, like reading.

But when it comes to things that don't come so easily for me (like reading and writing), I realized I have more of a closed mindset. I get overwhelmed and frustrated, and then I avoid doing the hard things and can't be gritty.

I lose motivation for my schoolwork even though I want to do well and make my parents and teachers proud. Sometimes I put a lot of pressure on myself because I want to get good grades like my friends, but when I don't I tend to catastrophize and have all-or-nothing thinking, which makes me feel even more stressed.

This year I've been using tools and strategies to help me stay organized. I'm really focusing on getting in the habit of writing down all of my assignments, putting my name and the date on every paper, and trying to keep my notebook organized. And I've been trying to read along while listening to audiobooks, draw summary pictures, and use sketches and color when I take notes. These things actually help me feel more on top of it all. I've learned that when I feel tired or overwhelmed, I get kind of cranky, so I try to get to bed on time. I try to get myself energized and focused when doing homework, but to be honest, sometimes I just feel tired and a little lazy after a long day at school, and rush through so I can be done.

Try to reflect on yourself honestly, and embrace that you are not perfect (no one is) and there are some things you are really good at and some that you could improve. If you need to refresh yourself on some of the concepts, here's a list of the main topics in each chapter:

- mindset and self-efficacy (Chapter 1)
- grit (Chapter 2)
- motivation, pressure, thinking errors (Chapter 3)
- navigating the school building and organizing materials (Chapter 4)
- learning and thinking style preferences (Chapter 5)
- active learning strategies (Chapter 6)
- executive functioning, organization, and self-monitoring (Chapter 7)
- stress, self-care, and coping strategies (Chapter 8)

Self-awareness is closely related to metacognition. When you are metacognitive, you use your own experiences and drive to plan how to handle new learning situations, check in with your understanding, and change your approach as you go along.

Try this exercise in metacognition and self-awareness:

 **Quiz**

Grab a piece of paper and a pencil and let's get started. Number your paper 1–9, and honestly consider how well you know yourself as you read each statement. Make note of whether you don't know, think you know, or definitely know this about yourself.

1. I know how I like to learn.

2. I know what motivates me.

3. I recognize when I need to use my resources.

4. I know what strategies have been most helpful for me in the past.

5. When I get stuck, I stop and think about what I already know.

6. If the first thing I try doesn't work, I know to try an alternative method.

7. When I need help, I know who to ask.

8. When I need help, I know specifically what to ask for help with.

9. I recognize when I am starting to feel stressed.

For any of them that you said "I don't know" or "I think I know," we encourage you to make a note of that and continue to practice being self-aware.

This self-quiz and this book might have been one of your first experiences being metacognitive, but it won't be your last! We don't expect you to be masters of self-awareness...yet. ☺ **WITH PRACTICE, MINDFULNESS, AND A GROWTH MINDSET, SELF-AWARENESS BECOMES MORE NATURAL AND HELPS YOU SELF-ADVOCATE.** But you can still advocate for yourself even if you aren't totally self-aware (yet) by being an active participant in your own learning.

 So, how do you self-advocate effectively?

Remember, self-advocacy means speaking up for yourself and making sure your needs are met. It includes asking for help and support or expressing your preferences. Self-advocacy is important for everyone. You may notice that your parents or other significant adults in your life do a lot of advocating for you, like talking to teachers, calling doctors, etc.

REALITY CHECK! Self-advocating is hard! Self-advocating is probably not something you prioritize as much as your schoolwork, but it's just as important, if not more! We understand that it usually doesn't come naturally and can feel uncomfortable or awkward. We've heard a lot of reasons for why kids don't self-advocate, like:

- They don't understand what self-advocating means.
- They don't know what they need.
- They don't know when they need something.
- They don't know they are allowed to ask or tell.
- They don't know who to ask or tell.
- They don't know how to explain what they need.
- They're embarrassed to ask or tell.
- They're worried they'll look stupid.
- They assume an adult will advocate for them.
- They're afraid they will make the person mad.
- They think asking for something they need isn't fair.
- They think it won't make a difference to ask because the teacher or adult will say no.

These aren't just excuses kids make to avoid taking responsibility: they're real concerns and reasons for feeling uncomfortable about speaking up for yourself. But once you understand why it's hard for you to self-advocate, you can challenge yourself by facing the discomfort and just doing it anyway.

EFFECTIVE AND INEFFECTIVE STRATEGIES FOR SELF-ADVOCACY

While you are being your own advocate, remember that it's still important to be kind and respectful to everyone—if you're rude, people may not want to listen to you. Communicate clearly and try to explain why you need what you're are asking for. If you can't explain, the other person may not understand. Self-advocacy is important for all aspects of your life, now and in the future.

Check out these examples of times when the crew needed to self-advocate. Each example has two scenarios: one where they didn't **effectively** self-advocate, and one where they did. Think about the differences between each, and why one method worked better than the other.

Take a Minute!

For each scenario, consider:

• Why was it important for the person to speak up and self-advocate?

• What impact could it have if they didn't speak up?

• How could you self-advocate in a similar situation?

We've answered the questions for you for Bryce's example—see if you can figure out the others on your own!

- **Why was it important for Bryce to speak up/ self-advocate?** She recognizes that both the audition and the project are important to her. She realizes that she does not have enough time to complete the project the way that she wants to and cannot change the date of the audition.

- **What impact could it have if she didn't speak up?** If she chose not to ask for the extension, Bryce would likely encounter more stress because of lack of time, and more pressure because she would feel like she is trying to do two things that are important at the same time.

- **How could you self-advocate if you were in a similar situation?** Do some advanced planning and if you find that there are too many things going on at one time, be proactive by talking to your teacher.

You can even self-advocate just for your own internal thoughts! For example, have you ever had a moment when you're sitting in class, trying to pay attention, but you just can't because you're overwhelmed? You might be stressing about a test, and homework, and after-school activities, and friend drama—you name it. You might be tempted to just put your head down and give up! Instead, try advocating for yourself and your need to take a minute to de-stress. Acknowledge your own feelings ("I'm feeling overwhelmed, and I need a minute to calm down"). Ask the teacher if you can have a moment to go get a drink of water, and use the time to take some deep breaths and clear your head.

There are lots of different ways that you can advocate, and some approaches will work better than others. And that's okay! Find what works best for you and your situation (it might be different every time!).

These are just a few examples where self-advocacy is helpful. Here are some other situations you might encounter:

- When you have four tests all scheduled for the same day

- When your teacher marks an answer wrong on your test, but you think your answer is correct

- When your parents want you to participate in a sport that you don't like

- When your friends want you to hang out or play a video game, but you have a test the next day

- When you had to stay home sick and you think it would help to have an extra day to complete your homework or project

- When your teacher moved on to the next slide but you missed some of the notes

- When the teacher asks if anyone has any questions, and you do

- When you missed some of the directions the teacher gave

- When you get skipped over for a team sport in PE

- When you're not given a chance to show your strengths during a sports tryout or audition

This list is just the tip of the iceberg of situations where you can self-advocate in middle school. And it'll be much easier to do later in life if you practice now. Everyone does better when they advocate for themselves in school, work, and personal relationships.

Everyone in middle school will need to self-advocate at some point, but we know that not everyone will need to advocate the same amount, depending on the situation and your environment. The need to self-advocate is affected by a person's circumstances, strengths, and weaknesses. In previous chapters, we've seen situations where students continue to struggle despite putting forth the effort, or continue to feel stressed or anxious even with coping strategies. If you encounter one of those situations, or have an official accommodation or learning plan at school, self-advocacy is particularly important to get what you need to be successful and feel comfortable. Check out the toolbox next for tools to help you build self-awareness and self-advocacy skills.

ASKING FOR HELP IS SOMETHING THAT WE ALL NEED TO DO SOMETIMES, AND KNOWING WHAT WE NEED AND HOW TO ASK FOR IT IS A STRENGTH, NOT A SIGN OF WEAKNESS.

 SELF-DETERMINATION TOOL BOX

TOOL #1: QUESTIONS TO GET YOURSELF UNSTUCK

Sometimes, it's hard to ask for help—you might not know exactly what you need or where to start when you feel "stuck." Exploring this is an excellent example of building self-awareness. When you catch yourself saying, "I don't know," or "I can't figure it out," give this tool a try.

Write down these questions on a sticky note (or put it in your phone's "notes" app). When you get stuck, read through the questions to help you work through the situation. Try to come up with a detailed answer for each question.

- Where am I stuck?
- What parts make sense to me?
- What are the parts I don't understand?

- What have I already tried?
- What do I think would be helpful?
- Who are the people that I could ask for help?

This self-questioning is designed to help you *understand* what you need. The next three tools will help you *express* what you need.

TOOL #2: GIVE YOURSELF A "LEG-UP"

It's important to be respectful when asking someone for help. Use this acronym (LEG-Up) to help you remember qualities that demonstrate respect.

- **L: Look** at the person you are talking to. It shows respect and that you take the conversation seriously (if you are uncomfortable making direct eye contact, at least look somewhere near their face).

- **E: Explain** the problem, how you have tried to fix it, what you are asking for, and the reason you are asking for it.

- **G: Give Gratitude** to the person for working with you and considering your request.

- **Up: Use** the accommodation you have been given.

TOOL #3: USE A TEMPLATE TO SELF-ADVOCATE IN WRITING ("BOING")

Just like advocating respectfully face-to-face, it is important to be polite and specific when you self-advocate in an email. Use this acronym (BOING) as a template to help you remember what to include in a respectful email:

- **(B)** Ask for what you need **Before** the deadline or due date.

- **(O)** Use a polite **Opening**.

- **(I)** Give **Information** about your plan or **Inquire** about what you need.

- **(N) Negotiate** for what is reasonable and will help you.

- **(G)** Show **Gratitude** by saying thank you before you sign your name.

From: Dillon@mainstreetschool.edu
To: mrjones@mainstreetschool.edu
Subject: Question About Grades
attachments: HistoryHW3.14, HistoryHW3.16, HistoryHW3.17

Dear Mr. Jones,

I was looking at my grades and realized that I am missing a few assignments. I think I turned in all of the homework from last week, but I don't see them in the portal yet. Just in case they got lost, I have attached copies of them to this email.

I know that I was absent on the day we had a quiz this week. Could I take it during lunch period on Thursday? Please let me know if that would be okay with you.

Thank you,
Dillon

TOOL #4: CREATE SUBTLE SYSTEMS

We know that speaking up for yourself during class can be tricky. While we encourage you to communicate with your teacher with your voice, we also understand that sometimes a non-verbal method is extremely helpful. It might help to meet privately with your teacher to create a way of communicating with them that works for you. It's basically making a plan with your teacher, even before you need it. Here are some examples that you could discuss with your teachers:

- Write a note at the top of your test before turning it in if you need more time.

- Put a green sticky note at the corner of your desk to let your teacher know when you need to leave the room for a stress or movement break.

- Put notes on your homework using a different color ink when you are unsure about the answer.

- Put a red sticky note on the corner of your desk to let the teacher know that you don't understand or need help.

- Use a sticky note on your homework to let your teacher know when you don't understand or have a question.

We hope you leave this last chapter with a stronger sense of being self-determined. Learning about yourself and how you think and feel is just as important as the knowledge the teachers give you every day. **BY BEING SELF-AWARE AND METACOGNITIVE, YOU CAN USE THE RIGHT TOOLS TO MEET YOUR GOALS AND MAKE IT EASIER TO BE IN MIDDLE SCHOOL.**

BUT DON'T STOP YOUR SELF-AWARENESS JOURNEY HERE! If you would like to learn more about anything we talked about in this book, hop on over to the Resources section, where you'll find some extra tools and references that can help you dive deeper into any of the topics.

We have thoroughly enjoyed going on this adventure with you and the crew.

~ANNA & BONNIE

EXTRA RESOURCES

We've put together a list of additional books, online resources, and mobile apps that we thought might help you and the adults in your life.

BOOKS FOR TWEENS AND TEENS

Baruch-Feldman, C. (2017). *The grit guide for teens: A workbook to help you build perseverance, self-control & a growth mindset*. Instant Help Books.

Boucher Gill, L. (2021). *Big brain book: How it works and all its quirks*. Magination Press.

Ciarrochi, J., Hayes, L., & Bailey, A. (2012). *Get out of your mind and into your life for teens: A guide to living an extraordinary life*. Instant Help Books.

Curley, P., & Parker, T. (2020). *Growth mindset workbook for kids: 55 fun activities to think creatively, solve problems, and love learning*. Rockridge Press.

Getz, L., & Prinstein, M. (2022). *Like ability: The truth about popularity*. Magination Press.

Langdon, M. (2021). *The hero handbook*. Magination Press.

Moss, W. L. (2021). *The friendship book*. Magination Press.

Moss, W. L., and DeLuca-Acconi, R. (2013). *School made easier: A kid's guide to study strategies and anxiety-busting tools*. Magination Press.

Pellegrino, K., & Sather, K. (2019). *Neon words: 10 Brilliant ways to light up your writing*. Magination Press.

Quinn, P. O., Stern, J. M., & Chesworth, M. (2001). *Putting on the brakes: Young people's guide to understanding attention deficit hyperactivity disorder (ADHD)*. Magination Press.

Schifrin, J. (2021). *The homework squad's ADHD guide to school success*. Magination Press.

Sperling, J. (2021). *Find your fierce: How to put social anxiety in its place*. Magination Press.

Tompkins, M. (2020). *Zero to 60: A teen's guide to manage frustration, anger, and everyday irritations*. Magination Press.

Tompkins, M. (2023). *Stress less: A teen's guide to a calm chill life*. Magination Press.

Zucker, B. (2022). *A perfectionist's guide to not being perfect*. Magination Press.

BOOKS FOR PARENTS, ADULT CAREGIVERS, AND TEACHERS

Duckworth, A. (2018). *Grit: The power of passion and perseverance* (Reprint ed.). Scribner.

Kenworthy, L., Anthony, L. G., Alexander, K. C., Adler Werner, M., Cannon, L. M., & Greenman, L. (2014). *Solving executive function challenges: Simple ways to get kids with autism unstuck and on target*. Paul H. Brookes Publishing Co.

Lavoie, R. D. (2008). *The motivation breakthrough: 6 secrets to turning on the tuned-out child*. Touchstone.

Paquette, J. (2018). *The happiness toolbox: 56 practices to find happiness, purpose & productivity in love, work and life.* Pesi Publishing & Media.

Sanguras, L. Y. (2017). *Grit in the classroom: Building perseverance for excellence in today's students.* Prufrock Press, Inc.

Stixrud, W. R., & Johnson, N. (2019). *The self-driven child: The science and sense of giving your kids more control over their lives.* Penguin Books.

Tough, P. (2013). *How children succeed: Grit, curiosity, and the hidden power of character.* Houghton Mifflin Harcourt.

VIDEOS AND PODCASTS

Being 12 Podcast: The Year Everything Changes. (2015). [Audio podcast]. WNYC. https://www.wnyc.org/series/being-12/

Big Life Journal Podcast: Big Life Kids podcast helps children develop a Growth Mindset. https://biglifejournal.com/pages/podcast

Cain, S. (2012,). *The power of introverts* [Video]. Ted Conferences. https://www.ted.com/talks/susan_cain_the_power_of_introverts

Duckworth, A. L. (n.d.) *Grit: The power of passion and perseverance* [Video]. TED Conferences. https://www.ted.com/talks/angela_lee_duckworth_grit_the_power_of_passion_and_perseverance

Noble, P. (2021). *Getting to know your brain: Dealing with stress* [Video]. NIMH. https://www.nimh.nih.gov/news/media/2021/getting-to-know-your-brain-dealing-with-stress

Smith, C., Daniels, M., & Beard, M. (Hosts). (2019–present). *Short & Curly* [Audio podcast]. Big Life Journal. https://www.abc.net.au/radio/programs/shortandcurly/

TED. (2014, December 17). *The power of believing that you can improve* | *Carol Dweck* [Video]. YouTube. https://www.youtube.com/watch?v=_XomgOOSpLU

Urban, T. (2016). *Inside the mind of a master procrastinator* [Video]. TED Conferences. https://www.ted.com/talks/tim_urban_inside_the_mind_of_a_master_procrastinator

ONLINE RESOURCES FOR TWEENS AND TEENS

The following websites include helpful and inspiring information that we hope you will enjoy.

THE BOUNCE BACK PROJECT: PROMOTING HEALTH THROUGH HAPPINESS

https://www.feelinggoodmn.org/what-we-do/bounce-back-project-
This initiative from CentraCare Health website offers information and ideas on the five pillars of resilience.

KIDSHEALTH.ORG

https:// www.kidshealth.org
This site has all sorts of information on kids' health, both physical and mental.

WHOLEHEARTED SCHOOL COUNSELING

https:// www.wholeheartedschoolcounseling.com

Trauma-informed and solution-focused resource maker for educators, parents, and students that focuses on social emotional learning, coping skills, and student success.

FAMOUS PEOPLE WITH LEARNING DIFFERENCES

An inspiring list of famous people with learning differences and/or AD/HD:
https://www.greatschools.org/gk/articles/famous-people-dyslexia-ld-or-ad-hd

ONLINE RESOURCES FOR ADULTS

Below are websites and organizations that we believe will be helpful for caregivers and other adults working with middle school kids.
https://www.kidshealth.org
https://www.ldaamerica.org
https://www.chadd.org
https://www.apa.org
https://www.ldonline.org

MOBILE APPS

Mobile apps are wonderful resources that can help kids and adults process their emotions or provide relaxation strategies. We hope you will explore some of these popular apps for additional support.

BEAR IN MIND

This app will help you create to-do lists and set up reminders to keep you on track with daily goals.

CALM

This app encourages mindfulness through guided meditations, movement sessions, music, and helpful tips. You can sort by goals like relaxation, productivity, focus, gratitude, sleep, etc.

CHOICEWORKS CALENDAR

This paid app is a great assistive technology tool that can alleviate the anxiety some kids associate with schedule changes. This app offers a picture-based learning tool that helps you learn what is happening day-to-day, week-to-week, and month-to-month throughout each year. It teaches the abstract concept of time in a structured visual format, which helps children organize their lives as well as understand sequence and time. This app provides a full-featured calendar designed with both the child and caregiver in mind.

CHORE PAD

This productivity app lets families set their own tasks or chores and supports creating a reward system based on completion.

HABITICA

This is a free habit-building and productivity app that treats your real life like a game. With in-game rewards and punishments to motivate you and a strong social network to inspire you, it can help you achieve your goals to become healthy, hard-working, and happy.

HABITZ

This app is fun to use and empowers you to develop healthy habits and stick to them.

HAPPIFY

Learn and practice activities that can help you combat negativity, anxiety, and stress while fostering positive traits like gratitude and empathy.

HAPPY NOT PERFECT

This app offers mind workouts, daily affirmations, and meditations to help you build confidence, manage stress, and promote sleep.

HEADSPACE

This app encourages mindfulness in your everyday life through thousands of guided meditations, as well as setting routines, reminders to take pauses, and active movement sessions.

INSIGHT TIMER

Thousands of different meditations, relaxing imagery and sounds, and guided practices, including ones specifically for anxiety and for bedtime, are offered on this free app.

STOP BREATH AND THINK

This subscription-based app helps you create a daily meditation practice and has meditations, journaling, videos, and even yoga lessons.

SMILING MIND

This not-for-profit guided meditation app was developed by psychologists and educators to help bring mindfulness into your life. It provides helpful instructional videos as well as programs customized by age that can be used in a variety of settings where one can benefit from mindfulness practice (home, school, work, sports, sleep, etc.).

STREAKS

This app helps you form or break habits and supports daily tracking by encouraging you not to break your streak.

SUPERBETTER

This mobile game is designed to improve the player's mental health and build resilience. It aims to help the user track their goals and achievements, while also providing education about the importance of each activity.

BIBLIOGRAPHY

CHAPTER 1

Bandura, A. (1977). Self-efficacy: Toward a unifying theory of behavioral change. *Psychological review, 84*(2), 191.

Dweck, C. S. (2006). *Mindset: The new psychology of success.* Random House.

CHAPTER 2

Duckworth, A. (2018). *Grit: The power of passion and perseverance* (Reprint ed.). Scribner.

Sanguras, L. Y. (2017). *Grit in the classroom: Building perseverance for excellence in today's students.* Prufrock Press, Inc.

CHAPTER 3

American Psychological Association. (2015, November 17). *Parents aiming too high can harm child's academic performance* [Press release]. https://www.apa.org/news/press/releases/2015/11/academic-performance

Bernstein, J. (2020, August 2). 7 thoughts that make children and teens feel miserable. *Psychology Today.* https://www.psychologytoday.com/us/blog/liking-the-child-you-love/202008/7-thoughts-make-children-and-teens-feel-miserable

Cherry, K. (2019, September 27). *Understanding Intrinsic Motivation.* Verywell Mind. https://www.verywellmind.com/what-is-intrinsic-motivation-2795385

Harpine, E. C. (2015). Is intrinsic motivation better than extrinsic motivation?. In *Group-Centered Prevention in Mental Health* (pp. 87-107). Springer, Cham.

Matosic, D., Ntoumanis, N., & Quested, E. (2016). Antecedents of need supportive and controlling interpersonal styles from a self-determination theory perspective: A review and implications for sport psychology research. *Sport and exercise psychology research*, 145-180.

Ryan, R. M., & Deci, E. L. (2000). Intrinsic and extrinsic motivations: Classic definitions and new directions. *Contemporary Educational Psychology*, 25(1), 54-67.

Stress. (2017). Nemours Teens Health. https://kidshealth.org/en/teens/stress.html#catrecipes

CHAPTER 4

Dantas, L. A., & Cunha, A. (2020). An integrative debate on learning styles and the learning process. *Social Sciences & Humanities Open*, 2(1), 100017. https://www.sciencedirect.com/science/article/pii/S2590291120300061

Pashler, H., McDaniel, M., Rohrer, D., & Bjork, R. (2008). Learning styles: Concepts and evidence. *Psychological science in the public interest*, 9(3), 105-119. https://www.psychologicalscience.org/journals/pspi/PSPI_9_3.pdf?fbclid=IwAR3mrRPDwQ7CwTBFZNIavKgQWGVuXzD8j_G3U4pymHnbvgjAknjMNVP9CdI

Willingham, D. T. (2018, May 29). *Ask the cognitive scientist: Does tailoring instruction to "learning styles" help students learn?* American Federation of Teachers. https://www.aft.org/ae/summer2018/ willingham?fbclid=IwAR3_PWWWVdawEYcqJz9fKDV_ eFlc6IlCt1U6ZsJ1nkoC6nH3wUcQGyGnWfo

CHAPTER 6

Boucher Gill, L. (2021). *Big brain book: How it works and all its quirks.* Magination Press.

Mcguire, S. Y., & McGuire, S. (2016). *Teach students how to learn: Strategies you can incorporate into any course to improve student metacognition, study skills, and motivation.* Stylus Publishing.

CHAPTER 7

Guare, R., Dawson, P., & Guare, C. (2013). *Smart but scattered teens: The "executive skills" program for helping teens reach their potential.* Guilford Press.

CHAPTER 8

American Psychological Association. (2018). *Stress in America: Generation Z.* https://www.apa.org/news/press/releases/ stress/2018/stress-gen-z.pdf

American Psychological Association. (2018, November 1). *Stress effects on the body.* https://www.apa.org/topics/stress/body

McEwen, B. S., & Gianaros, P. J. (2010). Central role of the brain in stress and adaptation: Links to socioeconomic status, health, and disease. *Annals of the New York Academy of Sciences, 1186,* 190.

National Institutes of Mental Health. (n.d.) *I'm so stressed out! fact sheet.* https://www.nimh.nih.gov/health/publications/so-stressed-out-fact-sheet

National Institutes of Mental Health. (2020). *The teen brain: 7 things to know.* https://www.nimh.nih.gov/health/publications/the-teen-brain-7-things-to-know

Ross, F. (2018, June 8). *Stress vs. anxiety – Knowing the difference is critical to your health.* Mental Health First Aid. https://www.mentalhealthfirstaid.org/external/2018/06/stress-vs-anxiety/

Tan, L., & Martin, G. (2015). Taming the adolescent mind: A randomised controlled trial examining clinical efficacy of an adolescent mindfulness-based group programme. *Child and Adolescent Mental Health, 20*(1), 49-55.

Zucker, B. (2016). *Anxiety-free kids: An interactive guide for parents and children* (2nd ed.). Routledge.

CHAPTER 9

Hui, E. K., & Tsang, S. K. (2012). Self-determination as a psychological and positive youth development construct. *The Scientific World Journal.*

Wehmeyer, M. L., Abery, B. H., Mithaug, D. E., & Stancliffe, R. J. (2003). *Theory in self-determination: Foundations for educational practice.* Charles C Thomas Publisher.

Wehmeyer, M. L., & Field, S. L. (2007). *Self-determination: Instructional and assessment strategies.* Corwin Press.

ACKNOWLEDGMENTS

We both would like to recognize several people without whom this book would not be possible.

To Kristine Enderle and Katie Ten Hagen: Kristine, thank you for developing this book series, and creating the opportunity for us to collaborate with this talented team of professionals. It has been an amazing experience. We could not think of a better way to expand our platform for sharing our passion for helping children and adolescents. Thank you, Katie, for also supporting our vision and helping make our ideas even better!

We would like to express our immense gratitude to Dr. Bonnie Zucker. Thank you for inviting us to be a part of this book series. Thank you for your kind and thoughtful guidance throughout this process. We have learned an incredible amount from you, and are so grateful that you were the series editor!

To our series team members, Dr. Lenka Glassman, Dr. Silvi Guerra, and, again, Dr. Bonnie Zucker: being a part of this team with you has been a wonderful experience and we are grateful to have been a part of the Kid Confident series team.

We would like to say how much we appreciate the love and support of our friends and family and take a moment to say a special thanks to a few very special people in our lives.

ANNA

To my mom and dad: I love you both very much. You have always encouraged me to be the best person I can be, and your selfless love, devotion, and passion for learning are inspiring. So much of who I am and what is included in this book stems from what I have learned from the two of you. I am forever grateful and blessed to be able to share this with you.

To my sister, Rachel: I am grateful for your love, compassion, and positive energy every day. Thank you for being the most supportive big sister anyone could ever ask for. I have tremendous gratitude for our amazing relationship—even when sisters can be mad or sad ☺—and I would never want it to stop. Love you!

To my husband, Tom: You were an inspiration throughout the process of writing this book, including some of the characters, having known you since our middle school years! I love you and our journey in this world together more than anything. I cannot thank you enough for your daily acts of kindness and love and for keeping me motivated—always with a contagious smile!

To my co-author, Bonnie: You influenced my education very early in life—since middle school! So many of my educational and career aspirations became a reality because of what you taught me, and I can never thank you enough for that. You will always be a mentor to me, and I am so happy to now call you a colleague and friend. I could not think of a better topic to write about together. Thank you for being such a wonderful co-author!

BONNIE

To my mom and dad: My whole life you have been my biggest supporters and greatest fans. Thank you for believing in me and knowing (even when I didn't) that who I was in middle school was not the version of me that I would one day become. You are my role models and my heroes, and I am so grateful for your support. I love you more.

To my husband, Joe: Thank you for supporting my career and "projects," even when they take time away from us. You are my best friend, and I couldn't imagine life without you. I love you like crazy.

To Anna: Who would have thought when we first met (when you were in middle school) that we would someday write a book together? I am so proud of all that you have accomplished since we met. I am beyond excited that we are now colleagues as well as friends. You are the best co-author anyone could ever ask for and I am so grateful you asked me to join you in this adventure!

To my friends and family: Thank you for sharing in my excitement and for your unconditional love and encouragement. I am grateful for each of you every single day.

To my students: I had all of you in mind as I wrote this book. I feel honored to have worked with each and every one of you and I hope that in some small way I had a positive impact on your school journey, because you certainly had a positive impact on me.

ABOUT THE AUTHORS

ANNA POZZATTI, PhD, is a psychologist in private practice at Bonnie Zucker & Associates in Rockville, MD. She has a strong clinical background in providing evidence-based treatments for children and adolescents. She utilizes cognitive-behavioral therapy (CBT), behaviorism, and a family systems approach to treat anxiety, OCD, and a variety of social, emotional, and behavioral challenges. She lives in Rockville, MD.

BONNIE MASSIMINO, MEd is a Board Certified Educational Therapist, certified Special Education teacher, and Reading Specialist with over 25 years of experience working with neurodiverse learners, specializing in supporting children and adults with learning disabilities, attention disorders, and executive functioning challenges. She lives in Olney, MD.

ABOUT THE ILLUSTRATOR

DEANDRA HODGE is an illustrator and designer based in Washington, DC. She received her Bachelor of Arts in Fine Arts, concentrating in Graphic Design from University of Montevallo. Visit @deandrahodge_ on Instagram.

KID CONFIDENT

1

KID CONFIDENT #1

"Smart and essential"
—Jeff Kinney,
Diary of a Wimpy Kid

HOW TO MASTER
SOCIAL POWER
IN MIDDLE SCHOOL

by Bonnie Zucker, PsyD • illustrated by DeAndra Hodge

"Guide for fostering a happy adolescence by maneuvering its challenges and pitfalls...The lively design, including playful illustrations, makes for accessible reading, with ideas unpacked into digestible pieces."—Kirkus

2

KID CONFIDENT #2

"Smart and essential"
—Jeff Kinney,
Diary of a Wimpy Kid

HOW TO MASTER
YOUR MOOD
IN MIDDLE SCHOOL

by Lenka Glassman, PsyD • illustrated by DeAndra Hodge

"An excellent mental health resource for adolescents and those who support them...illustrations and diagrams support the text, making subjects... more accessible...Packed with valuable material, this volume is an informative read for middle schoolers who struggle with their emotions." —Kirkus

3

KID CONFIDENT #3

"Smart and essential"
—Jeff Kinney,
Diary of a Wimpy Kid

HOW TO HANDLE
STRESS
FOR MIDDLE SCHOOL SUCCESS

by Silvi Guerra, PsyD • illustrated by DeAndra Hodge

4

KID CONFIDENT #4

"Smart and essential"
—Jeff Kinney,
Diary of a Wimpy Kid

HOW TO
NAVIGATE
MIDDLE SCHOOL

by Anna Pozzatti, PhD, & Bonnie Massimino, MEd. illustrated by DeAndra Hodge